CAN'T-LOSE ACCOUNTS

Can't-Lose Accounts

DELIVER VALUE AND MAKE IT SIMPLE TO RENEW AND BUY MORE!

Steve Thompson

VALUE LIFECYCLE™

CAN'T-LOSE ACCOUNTS

Deliver Value and Make It Simple to Renew and Buy More!

ISBN   978-1-5445-3137-3 *Paperback*

        978-1-5445-3138-0 *Ebook*

Contents

Foreword

Author's Note: The manuscript for this book was completed prior to the COVID-19 pandemic and subsequent lockdowns. Because of COVID, I toyed with revising references to face-to-face meetings to reflect the nuances of virtual meetings. However, with halting but hopeful progress toward reopening and the eventual resumption of in-person business meetings, I decided to leave the context as is. All that said, whether our meetings are in-person or online, the same principles and concepts apply.

Meet Bob.

Bob is in a pickle.

A sales associate at a successful technology company, Bob's problem began two months ago when his largest customer,

Acme Brands, hired a new chief financial officer (CFO) to help speed up growth and improve financial performance. Bob had noticed that Acme's stock performance was not what their CEO had been promising Wall Street, but he didn't think they were in any real trouble, at least not to the extent it would impact him directly. Now he wasn't so sure.

About a year ago, Bob sold Acme a sizable deal as a "pilot" in one of their six divisions. The assumption was that if things went well, he would be offered the remaining five divisions. As a matter of routine, after the initial award, Bob turned the account over to his internal teams to manage implementation and customer retention. He then turned his attention to finding new opportunities at other accounts. Acme, he reasoned, was well taken care of. But while his year had started off strong, heading into the fourth quarter, Bob's sales numbers were beginning to lag, and he was now pinning his hopes on reaching this year's quota by winning that follow-on business at Acme's other five divisions.

Last week, however, Acme's new CFO put all current initiatives on hold pending a thorough review. This put a stop to the new statement of work (SOW) Bob had been developing for the other five divisions with his primary contact, Tara, and her team. This SOW, which represented nearly his entire sales pipeline, was now on hold indefinitely—and there was nothing he could do about it!

To make matters worse, today the CFO pulled Tara (who was also Bob's biggest champion) into a financial review meeting. In the meeting, the CFO pulled out a spreadsheet with the total billings from Bob's company to date and said to Tara, "We're spending a lot of money with these guys. What value have we gotten from them for what we've spent so far?"

Tara's rushed boilerplate responses of "Everything is going great" and "We're happy with their performance" didn't satisfy the CFO, and he gave her one week to come back with a detailed analysis of the real value Bob's company had delivered to the business. What Bob had believed to be a good relationship (and plan) was now turning decidedly sour as Tara just gave him three days to come up with a value-delivered statement and present it to Acme.

Fast forward a couple of days. In a hard scramble, Bob and his team have pulled together the value he believes his firm has delivered. First, the technology has met all their technical specifications as demonstrated in the proof of concept. Second, he gave them a significant discount to help close the deal before quarter end. Third, the solution was performing in production just like it did in the POC. Finally, the solution was delivered on time and on budget. Bob sent the report to Tara this morning, but now it's late afternoon, and she has yet to respond to his phone calls and emails.

What just happened to Bob? You might argue that a new CFO coming on board and subjecting every spend to intense scrutiny was hardly predictable. But what was *entirely predictable* was Bob's eventual need to do more than deliver the promised value to his customer. He needed to get credit for his company's Past Value Delivered (PVD). For the new CFO at Acme, this would both justify the initial purchase and the planned future purchases for the remaining divisions. But it looks like Bob's team has confused what Acme bought (better outcomes) with what they paid for (his products and services). If you've read the four preceding books in this Value Lifecycle™ series (or even just a couple of them), you'll know that Bob's last-minute hustle to provide critical value messaging to key customer stakeholders is far too common a scenario.

We deliver value and then get credit for that value in order to retain customers and win more business (the main objectives of account management). But we also do it to protect the people who awarded us the business in the first place—the key decision makers who are often under the gun and at significant political risk for their decision to bring in a supplier and their solutions. We must help them look like "heroes" in their organizations by documenting and reporting the important outcomes and the value their decisions have brought to their business. We may bemoan how difficult it is to sell large, complex deals, but in turn, we should always remember how difficult it is for the customer to buy—and then demonstrate internally that they made a good business decision.

If there is one theme I hope you've embraced throughout the *Must-Win Deals* series, it is this:

It's all about the customer and what's important to them (outcomes) while minimizing the risk of uncertainty for you and the customer.

In this book, we will explore the primary cause of risk and uncertainty: *change*. With sales cycles of six to nine months (or longer) for complex B2B deals—not to mention the months it can take to deploy a typical solution before the customer can really start to see meaningful results—change, and the disruption it brings, is inevitable.

This book, the fifth and final volume in the *Must-Win Deals* series, explores delivering (and getting credit for) the promised value and how doing so makes renewals simple, referrals enthusiastic, and upselling and cross-selling opportunities much more bountiful. The first book in the series, *Must-Win Deals*, reveals the four common things we, as sellers, do to make it challenging for customers to award us key deals. It also explores the idea of pursuing not just any deal, but a Great Deal. *The Irresistible Value Proposition* then reveals how to develop a Value Proposition that gets the customer excited about doing business with us right now. Book three, *The Compelling Proposal*, showcases the proposal as a strategic tool to reinforce trust and credibility, making it easier for the customer to buy from us (and sell internally), while managing the uncertainty inherent in the real world. Next, *The Painless Negotiation* shows how to negotiate effectively by first ensuring we are having the "right negotiation" and then negotiating the "right way." Our goal as sellers should always be to close a great deal—one that is good for us and the customer—with key deal levers that increase the odds that we can work together to deliver the promised value. I hope you have personally derived great value from this journey!

To be sure, change can bring both positive and negative outcomes. One decidedly negative outcome, and one that you must proactively manage, is risk to your current engagement (and, thus, to your customer's key decision makers). On the positive side, and just as important to your long-term success, are new opportunities to sell that change can create. Although we've encountered "the 'o' word" often in this series, until now we haven't answered a fundamental question: What generates an *opportunity*? And if "change" is the answer (or at least one very important answer), then how do you "hunt for" change when you're selling?

In simple terms, you should be hunting for changes in the customer's business. This is where opportunities tend to "hide in plain sight." Is the customer changing their go-to-market strategy? Are they launching new products or services? Are they looking to acquire companies to expand their business and their offerings? Are they considering expansion into international markets? Perhaps they are looking to divest low-growth or unprofitable business lines. Or maybe they are entering into new strategic alliances with other firms. What about changes at the top levels of the organization? These are just a few examples of the types of changes that create new opportunities. And they all have one thing in common: the company is typically prepared to commit resources (especially money) to address each of these potential changes!

If you're like me, you'd rather try to sell into situations where you know the company is committing money and resources. That's where I've done my largest deals. Think about it: every customer (current or prospective) does business in a world of change. Perhaps the only businesses or business-like entities that can operate in a static environment are the government (until there is a political change), monopolies supported and protected by the government (until the laws change), and utilities (until regulations change). For everyone else, change is a constant driver of growth and opportunity. From regulatory changes to fast-evolving technology to competitive pressures to novel solutions, companies must adapt to the change(s) they are up against, and that is where our opportunities lie.

As simple as this concept seems, salespeople (and their management) desperate for pipeline still gravitate to the same old playbook, calling on the same customer contacts, looking for funded "projects" they can sell into. Another tired tactic is going after market share and unseating incumbents with "blue light special" pricing. But this hit-and-miss, "non-strategic" play invariably leads to competitive retaliation. After all, *your* key customers can just as easily (and unimaginatively) be targeted with rock-bottom pricing. As this plays out, you and your competitors will likely end up where you started, only poorer because now you've done nothing to change your market share, and you've driven all the margin out of the market.

Another theme of the *Must-Win Deals* series I hope I've brought home is that a robust, qualified sales pipeline will alleviate more than 90 percent of all sales issues. And by far the easiest sale in the world is to an existing, *happy* customer. Yet many salespeople will quickly exit an account after they've booked the business and go looking for new opportunities with other accounts. After all, they're being paid to "hunt" for new logos, not "farm" existing accounts. As Bob's story above illustrates, this may work for a while—until it doesn't.

And let's not forget about the costs to the business of acquiring new customers versus keeping the ones you have. Forbes estimates that landing a new customer may cost up to five times more than keeping an existing one happy and ready to buy more.[1] Baine & Company calculate that just

---

1   Jia Wertz, "Don't Spend 5 Times More Attracting New Customers, Nurture the Existing Ones," *Forbes*, September 12, 2018, https://www.forbes.com/sites/jiawertz/2018/09/12/dont-spend-5-times-more-attracting-new-customers-nurture-the-existing-ones/#4408ddd45a8e

a 5-percent increase in customer retention can drive an increase in profits from 25–95 percent, depending on the nature of the business.[2] Invesp found that the probability of selling to an existing customer is 60–70 percent while the probability of selling to a new customer is only 5–20 percent.[3]

Clearly, keeping and selling to existing customers is the better path toward robust pipeline, and the best companies and sales organizations realize this. New opportunities continually manifest as existing customers' businesses change and evolve. If you happen to have a customer whose business is entirely static and nothing is changing, then there are no opportunities for you to sell. The good news is that for most companies *something is always changing*, creating opportunities for us and providing justification for keeping sales involved *after the sale* to continue growing the customer.

But to capitalize on the opportunities generated by change, you must first ensure that you have delivered the promised value from prior purchases and that the *customer has given*

2   Fred Reichheld, "Prescription for Cutting Costs," *Bain & Company*, http://www2.bain.com/Images/BB_Prescription_cutting_costs.pdf.

3   Khalid Saleh, "Customer Acquisition vs. Retention Costs—Statistics and Trends," Invesp, last modified November 11, 2019, https://www.invespcro.com/blog/customer-acquisition-retention.

you credit for delivering that value. How can you ensure that you remain relevant to the customer's key decision makers and that new change-driven opportunities are freely presented to you?

You need a plan to deliver the value—a Customer Success Plan that addresses all the common issues that put accounts at risk.

CHAPTER 1

Delivering the Value

What Your Customer Wanted All Along

To set the stage for exploring how to keep and grow "can't-lose" accounts, let's look at what puts these accounts at risk in the first place. Three things could influence your customer's decision *not* to buy from you again and will draw a bead on what you need to manage *after* you win the business. Basically, accounts churn because:

→ **Technical Challenges** have affected the implementation of your solution (or perhaps you sold the wrong solution).

→ The customer does not perceive your **Past Value Delivered** (PVD).

→ *Changes* within your customer's business have put your engagement at risk.

The first bullet point is outside the scope of this book, and we're going to assume that your company is very good at implementing your solutions and that the solutions "perform as advertised." (If not, you've got a business problem that will result in sales and account management issues down the road.)

But even if you've rolled your solution out without a hitch, you may still lose your customer's repeat business if they are unaware of the past value you have delivered. **Past Value Delivered** is more than just another TLA (three-letter acronym). If you've gone to the trouble (and expense) of winning the business, the best insurance you can buy is helping your customer understand and articulate the *value* your solution delivered. After all, among the three key risk factors to keeping accounts, this is likely the one over which you have the most control. Take time to educate your contact(s) and any key stakeholders in the account on the business value of your solution—that is, the net outcomes your solution brought to their business that were incrementally better than any other options they may have considered. Don't get caught out scrambling to put this together when you're asked to justify the cost of a past solution you delivered. Instead, it should be as easy as picking up the phone and having your customer deliver the value message for you.

Finally, at the moment you sign a deal with a customer, changes that will affect their business are already in motion. Some changes will happen quickly; others will take more time. Some will have minimal impact on your relationship; others, significantly more. And while you may not be able to predict what those changes may be, you can be certain that change will happen. It is the *only* constant in business, which is why it continues to mystify me that so many sales and account management processes don't account for and manage the risk and uncertainty surrounding change. This too will be a significant topic of this book.

The two things you can and must proactively do something about after the sale:

1. Ensure the value gets delivered (and you get credit).

2. Ensure you have the right processes in place to manage change.

First things first. Let's turn our attention back to the value the customer has been seeking since your first engagement with them and take a deeper dive into the second bullet in our "risk list."

PAST VALUE DELIVERED (PVD)

Let's say you just landed a huge contract. Congratulations! You worked hard to create the potential for value for your customer, you presented an irresistible value proposition, then delivered a compelling proposal—and now you've captured that value in a great deal through your negotiation efforts. You've booked the business, exceeded your quota, and cashed the commission check. Time to party, right?

Sure, but not too hard, for the most important phase of the Value Lifecycle™ is yet to come, and you need to be *on your game*. It's worth highlighting here that while this fifth and final book contains about 20 percent of the *Must-Win Deals* series content, from the customer's perspective that number should be about 90 percent. And if you've read carefully, by now you'll have picked up a concept that runs like bedrock below the Lifecycle: when it comes to creating value, you should be thinking like your customer! Another way to think about it: you and your company need sales pipeline from your customers; your customers need (and will demand) value from you.

It follows then that from your very first sales motion with any customer, whether for new or repeat business, you should be focusing on how you are going to deliver value to them—value that can be quantified, that your customer can articulate, and that you can then use to help ensure that your customer seeks you out for more business, helping to keep that pipeline full and healthy. This is why the Value Lifecycle™ is circular (and why *Value* is half the name). And the biggest single driver of that circularity is change—change within the customer's business that can create new opportunities. With a constant eye out for change, our job then is to use it to *proactively* drive the cycle.

For too many sales organizations, however, the sales team bows out at exactly the point where they should be concerned with *delivering* and *getting credit for* the value they have just created and captured for their customer. I believe this is a grave mistake.

Let's have another look at Figure 1.1 (which you may know by heart by now).

DELIVERING VALUE AND GETTING CREDIT
Managing Value After the Sale

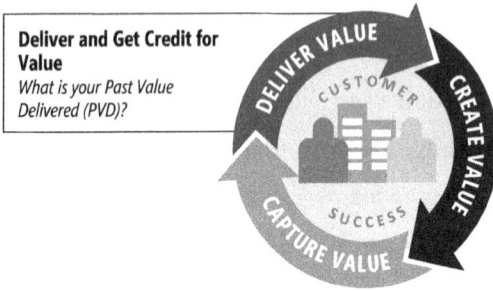

Deliver and Get Credit for Value

What is your Past Value Delivered (PVD)?

DELIVER VALUE

CREATE VALUE

CAPTURE VALUE

CUSTOMER

SUCCESS

Figure 1.1

Many of my buying clients think of what transpires before a deal is closed as the "sausage making" of the ongoing relationship. They like the outcome (the value they receive), but nobody's all that interested in the details of how they got it (how that value was created or captured). Here, in the final phase of the Value Lifecycle™, your customers want you to deliver the "sausage"—the value you promised. And believe it or not, they are prepared to give you credit for that delivery. Why? Because giving you credit for delivering value *makes them look smart* for choosing your company and your solution over the alternatives. Remember, by this time, the customer has participated in the sausage making by committing a huge amount of time, effort, and financial resources, and they expect better outcomes. When you are not there to get credit for the Past Value Delivered, you miss the best part of the process and leave a huge amount of future pipeline potential on the table.

But credit for PVD is not only important to key decision makers; it bears directly on future sales success. Both with the same customer and *between* customers, Past Value Delivered is used to:

→ Provide enthusiastic references that are truly impactful and relevant

→ Justify continuing to do business with you (renewals)

→ Support awarding more business to you (upsell/ cross-sell)

Past Value Delivered is also critical to the *long-term success* of your business. Recent research by Gartner into why accounts fail to grow[4] yields some crucial insights, as shown in Figure 1.2.

4   Kelly Blum, "Position Sales Teams to Grow Accounts, Not Just Retain Them," Gartner, December 21, 2018, https://www.gartner.com/smarterwithgartner/ position-sales-teams-to-grow-accounts-not-just-retain-them.

WHY EXISTING ACCOUNTS DON'T GROW

What if we provide a successful product and great service?
- Customers are twice as likely to renew versus an unsuccessful product or poor service.
- Customers are **no more likely** to buy more (upsell, cross-sell, etc.) than if the product or service experience was bad.

What then drives customer growth?
- The greatest driver of growth is delivering improved *outcomes* to the customer, which **equally** drives renewals.

Source: Gartner, 2019, *Why Accounts Aren't Growing.*

Figure 1.2

When you provide a successful product or service, customers are twice as likely to renew with you than when they receive poor service or when your solution fails to perform. Renewals are important, so this is a good thing. But what about growing the account through upselling and cross-selling? After all, it makes sense that an existing, happy customer would promote your solutions and good service to other units within their company, right? Wrong. According to Gartner's research, even when you provide a successful product or service (which performs as advertised), customers are *no more likely* to buy more from you through upselling or cross-selling than when their experience is negative.

Read that again as this is a crucial insight into the thinking of businesses that buy from you. You can bend over backwards to deliver a great solution, and this may increase the likelihood of *renewals* for that specific solution, but it does not mean that your customer will promote you within their company, resulting in cross-selling and upselling opportunities. You have simply satisfied the threshold of what they paid for (your products or services), but you have not met the threshold of what the customer bought (improved outcomes).

To help get your head around this important threshold between renewals and growth, it may help to think like a buyer. Let's say you're buying something online and you find what looks like the right product at the right price that can be delivered on time. The terms of your satisfaction are simple. You expect simple execution, and that means the product must be exactly what you ordered (not a cheap knock-off), it must arrive in good shape (no shipping damage or missing parts), and it must arrive when promised.

If all these criteria are met, the next time you need that product, you are likely to simply repeat that buying process with the same vendor. Or you may go an extra step and sign up to receive regular delivery. The seller met your minimum threshold of customer satisfaction, and you are likely to reward them with renewed business (at some future date). But just clearing that minimum threshold is unlikely to motivate you to promote that seller to your friends. This is why getting beyond the renewals threshold is about more than just executing in the technical delivery of your solutions. Your renewal purchase may simply be motivated by convenience or even pure inertia. It's just not worth it to spend time looking for a better, faster, or cheaper solution. In short, you are satisfied.

So, what drives customer growth? How do you break through that threshold that keeps a customer—even a demonstrably satisfied one—from talking to other stakeholders in their company about that great solution that you flawlessly delivered? One word: *outcomes*. Customers are driven to buy more from you when you deliver on their desired outcomes. Simply put, Past Value Delivered drives customer retention *and growth*.

MAKE CHANGE WORK FOR YOU

Change is a blade that cuts both ways. It is an engine for creating new opportunities, but it can also lead to unexpected customer churn. According to AskForensics[5], the number one factor that puts an existing account at risk is a supplier failing to proactively provide recommendations and solutions to *changing* and evolving customer needs.

Consider a situation where a key decision maker and/or champion in your customer's business leaves their position, perhaps for another company. Sitting down with their replacement and detailing what you've been doing and the past value you've delivered to the business will put you and your company in a wholly different light in the eyes of this new individual. Not only will it helpfully set you apart from other suppliers, it will also likely put you near the top of the list of companies your new contact will want to discuss their *new plans* with (and we know that new people almost always have new plans). The same applies when turnover affects your company. With well-documented PVD, the new sales or account rep can get up to speed quickly on *what* the customer has paid for in the past (products and services) and, more importantly, *why* they spent their money with you (their desired outcomes and value) and the *value you've delivered* to date. How many times have you taken over an existing account and wished you had half those insights?

5   AskForensics, "2020 B2B Sales Analysis: Top Hidden Customer Expectations Causing B2B Accounts to Defect,"January 20, 2020.

DROPPING THE BATON

All too often, however, I see companies make it virtually impossible for this scenario to play out. Instead, sales organizations "close the folder" and hand over their hard-won accounts to Implementation Services, Operations, Support, Renewals, Customer Success, and other internal teams to do all the implementation and follow-up. What happens to all the hard-earned insights into outcomes, success metrics, and the value the customer expects from the purchase? How is this transmitted clearly to the very people that are expected to deliver it? Too often it is not, and the salespeople who may know it are a thousand miles away, figuratively and possibly literally. This value delivery gap greatly reduces the likelihood that the selling company will have a clear view of the outcomes and value the customer expects. This increases the likelihood that the promised value (success) will not be delivered.

Many companies subcontract large parts of this phase to a channel partner. Here the risks are the same or even magnified. To be clear, there is nothing inherently wrong with "passing the baton," whether internally or to a fulfillment partner. Salespeople, after all, are good at selling, and people involved in delivery and fulfillment services are best suited for what they do. But who then is responsible for ensuring that everyone in the organization is focused on achieving the promised outcomes and delivering on the success metrics (value)? In short, sales should be responsible for ensuring that the "baton" is successfully passed by developing a cohesive Customer Success Plan that will help the new owner of the customer relationship deliver the promised value and remain relevant to the customer (especially the key decision makers). The objective is not just a satisfied customer but rather a *successful* customer that will readily offer up potential new opportunities when things invariably change.

THE CUSTOMER SUCCESS PLAN

You may have a different name for the Customer Success Plan (CSP). (I've seen "Joint Business Plan," "Engagement Plan," and "Value Delivery Plan," to name a few.) But regardless of what you call it, your CSP should always be the centerpiece of a formal kickoff meeting shortly after you close a deal. This meeting should be attended by customer key decision makers as well as those charged with the day-to-day management of the engagement—from both the seller and the buyer[6]. To be clear, this is not the same as a

---

6 Like all the other key concepts in this series, the Customer Success Plan, to be most effective, must be a *collaborative effort* between the seller and buyer. Both sides must "own it" and be committed to achieving its purpose.

project plan, which is a subset of the CSP and tends to be more technical in nature. Table 1.1 details the four simple components of an effective Customer Success Plan.

Customer Success Plan Outline

- Finalize the outcomes and metrics for success (value) in a **Scorecard** designed to capture Past Value Delivered.

- Develop a high-level **Implementation Plan** with milestones and responsibilities (Gantt chart), detailing how we will achieve our goals.

- Capture and manage changes that may present risk or innovations that could bring new value opportunities in a forward-looking **Changes and Innovations** table.

- Establish a **Communications Plan** to report progress (daily, weekly, monthly) and drive Customer Value Reviews.

Table 1.1

The Customer Success Plan is a simple and logical extension of the Compelling Proposal you presented to the customer.

It should begin with a title that captures the overarching outcomes that are important to the customer (see Figure 1.3 from our Case Story). As you will recall, the proposal invited the customer to help construct the "right deal" to support the specific outcomes they wanted to achieve and thus establish what they were buying (outcomes) and what they were paying for (the right products and services). The Customer Success Plan, which the customer jointly develops with you, lays out *how* you will achieve those desired outcomes and *when* they should be achieved as well as how you will communicate your progress.

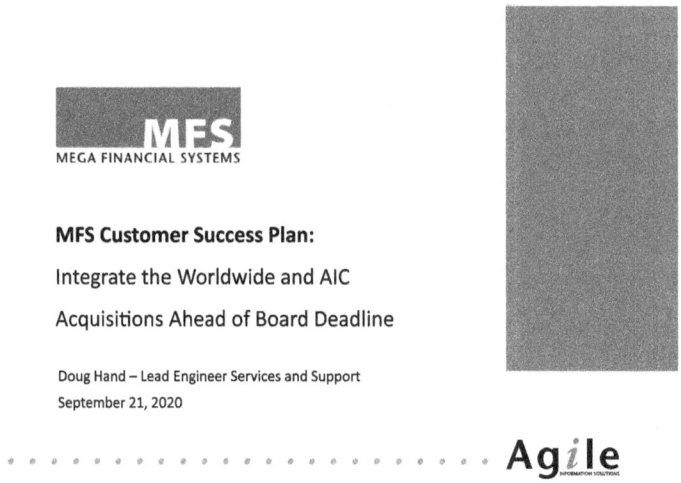

MEGA FINANCIAL SYSTEMS

MFS Customer Success Plan:
Integrate the Worldwide and AIC
Acquisitions Ahead of Board Deadline

Doug Hand – Lead Engineer Services and Support
September 21, 2020

Ag*i*le

Figure 1.3

The Scorecard

Let's explore the elements of the CSP, starting with the Scorecard. If you've been selling to customer outcomes all along, then finalizing those outcomes, due dates, and success metrics should be nothing more than documenting what each side has already discussed and agreed to. It may also include modifications to certain items to address changes that may have occurred late in the sales cycle. Either way, both sides should collaborate and agree on the targets they are aiming for.

The Scorecard is a straightforward and concise way to mark status and progress toward achieving the outcomes. Its simple format gives executives a way to quickly grasp the current situation and drill down on areas that may need their attention. The best Scorecards are also interactive and easy to access and act on by both your customer and your organization, with data that can be added and updated by both parties. It should serve as the *single point of truth* for delivering the promised value.

Figure 1.4 shows the Scorecard developed for the kickoff meeting between MFS and Agile in the Case Story.

Focus Areas	Outcomes / Metrics	Value Delivered	Notes / Action Items
Worldwide / MFS Integration	Compile and Reformat MFS Account Data by 10/12/20		
	Import MFS Account Data by 10/19/20		
	Rebrand Worldwide Platform, Portal, and Interfaces to MFS by 10/23/20		
	Train MFS Sales on Worldwide Platform, Portal, and Interfaces by 10/24/20		
	MFS IT Manage Agile Platform by 11/2/20		
	Go Live (100% Uptime) by 10/26/20		
AIC Integration	Compile and Reformat AIC Account Data by 11/2/20		
	Import AIC Account Data by 11/9/20		
	Complete "Hot Updates" – Zero Downtime		
	AIC Go Live on MFS by 11/9/20		

Figure 1.4

The Implementation Plan

The Implementation Plan documents high-level, interim milestones and phases. Most selling organizations tend to view this as a net new task after the sale—and react accordingly—but I'm seeing more and more buying organizations require that some type of Implementation Plan (as well as a Scorecard or something similar) be completed *before* they will issue a purchase order. So, if you are tempted to think of this as another procedural lemon, think *lemonade* instead. A thoughtful and thorough Implementation Plan will *increase* customer investment in the sale by lowering their perceived risk of doing business with you. The steps should be laid out in a timeline (such as a Gantt chart) with a single point of contact for the buyer *and* seller, someone assigned to be responsible for each phase or milestone. This is important, as everyone on both sides needs to know who they can reach out to and hold accountable for results and when issues and changes arise—as they almost certainly will.

Figure 1.5 shows the initial Implementation Plan for MFS and Agile.

MFS Implementation Plan															Ag*i*le
	#Days	Week 9/7	Week 9/14	Week 9/21	Week 9/28	Week 10/5	Week 10/12	Week 10/19	Week 10/26	Week 11/2	Week 11/9	Week 11/17	Week 11/23
Worldwide	42 days									2-Nov			
Compile Data	17 days			26-Sep			12-Oct						
Import Data	3 days						16-Oct	19-Oct					
Rebrand MFS	10 days						13-Oct	23-Oct					
Train Sales	5 days							19-Oct	24-Oct				
MFS IT Manage	35 days			28-Sep						2-Nov			
Go Live	1 day								★				
AIC	23 days						17-Oct				9-Nov		
Compile Data	14 days						19-Oct			2-Nov			
Import Data	6 days								3-Nov		9-Nov		
Hot Updates	2 days								26-Oct	28-Oct			
Go Live	1 day										★		
				9/21/2020 Kickoff							9-Nov		

Figure 1.5

Changes and Innovations

Managing change is bound to be one of the most challenging aspects of any implementation after the sale. Sometimes changes present issues for the engagement that must be addressed quickly and effectively. Other changes may be borne out of what is learned in the initial phases of the implementation, and these changes may provide opportunities to improve the plan, make things easier to accomplish, or produce better results. Finally, the seller may introduce new or improved versions of relevant products or services during the implementation, and these could have a positive bearing on the implementation and outcomes if incorporated. Regardless of the source, changes must be effectively managed.

Figure 1.6 shows the Agile and MFS Changes and Innovations portion of the Customer Success Plan.

Changes and Innovations			Ag*i*le

Focus Areas	Change / Innovation	Responsible (Agile & MFS)	Action Items
Changes			
Innovations			

Figure 1.6

The Communications Plan

One of the most overlooked elements of a Customer Success Plan is the Communications Plan, which details when both sides should meet and who should attend those meetings. A successful implementation will generally call for meetings that are technical, tactical, and strategic, and each type of meeting will likely happen at different frequencies and require different attendees. Daily or weekly meetings are likely to be more technical or tactical in nature, involving implementation staff, whereas monthly check-ins are going to be more strategic, calling for managers and sometimes executive attendance. Most complex implementations require that both buyer and seller communicate progress on a structured and regular basis, and a well-crafted Communications Plan is an important tool for raising and resolving execution issues.

Figure 1.7 shows the Agile and MFS Communications Plan presented at the kickoff meeting.

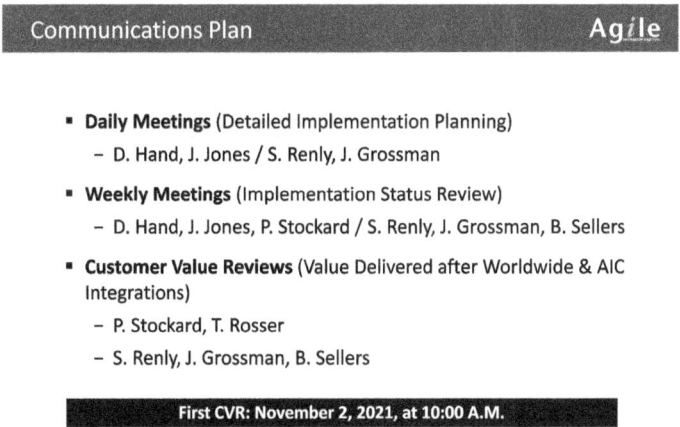

Communications Plan	Ag*i*le

- **Daily Meetings** (Detailed Implementation Planning)
  - D. Hand, J. Jones / S. Renly, J. Grossman
- **Weekly Meetings** (Implementation Status Review)
  - D. Hand, J. Jones, P. Stockard / S. Renly, J. Grossman, B. Sellers
- **Customer Value Reviews** (Value Delivered after Worldwide & AIC Integrations)
  - P. Stockard, T. Rosser
  - S. Renly, J. Grossman, B. Sellers

First CVR: November 2, 2021, at 10:00 A.M.

Figure 1.7

Remember, your goal is not just to implement your solution; you must also ensure that you have delivered the value you promised *and get credit for delivering that value* (Past Value

Delivered)—especially from the people who matter. For that, you should conduct formal Customer Value Reviews (CVRs) with your customer's key decision makers. CVRs must cover topics that are important enough for these stakeholders to justify investing their precious time. This is why your Customer Success Plan focuses foremost on the outcomes and value these individuals are keen to achieve and is the basis for any Customer Value Review, which we will explore in the next chapter.

I'm often asked when the ideal time is to develop the Customer Success Plan during the sales process. Ideally, the CSP should be jointly developed as soon as possible after contract award, followed by the formal kickoff meeting. However, I have clients who have successfully built the CSP into the latter stages of their sales cycle. Once a customer has settled on the "right deal" for them (see The Compelling Proposal) and in effect made it "their deal," it's natural to involve them in jointly developing the plan for successfully delivering the promised value. In short, the CSP should follow on the heels of a compelling proposal, when the customer is fully invested in both closing the deal and launching the implementation as soon as possible. I have seen this approach result in higher conversion rates and shorter sales cycles, outcomes that are good for both sellers and buyers!

CHAPTER 2

Getting Credit for Past Value Delivered

If You Don't, It Doesn't Really Count

Your business is selling, and you want to be presented with new opportunities to deliver value, ensuring that your sales pipeline is always growing. So, how do you ensure you are actively cultivating a "happy" customer—one that is receptive to giving you more business? When my selling clients diligently work to receive credit for Past Value Delivered, their sales pipelines typically grow 10–15 percent from upsell and cross-sell opportunities in their existing accounts, and their opportunities are three to five times more likely to close than net new business. After many years working with both selling and buying organizations, I have found that by far the best way to get credit for Past Value Delivered is to consistently use a simple, powerful process called Customer Value Review (CVR).

To be clear, a CVR is not a project review (or a technical review). If you are engaged in a project implementation, then you will be doing project reviews, meeting to evaluate milestones and deliverables. These are important, but they are focused on the "stuff" you promised to deliver (products and services) and the agreed delivery schedule. In many instances project reviews are conducted with lower-level contacts tasked with bringing what the customer "paid for" in on time and on budget. In my experience, most companies do a reasonably good job conducting project reviews.

The CVR, by contrast, is about *delivering the mutually agreed business outcomes* that the key decision makers wanted to achieve. Key objectives of the CVR are getting credit for the value you have delivered and uncovering new opportunities. As such, you should conduct these reviews with top stakeholders on the buyer's side. When do you start? As a rule, your first CVR should take place after the implementation is complete and your customer has had sufficient time using your products or services (or both) to start seeing the outcomes they were looking for. This means that the values for their key success metrics will be available to share—values that you will capture during the meeting. After the initial meeting, you can schedule follow-ups every quarter or twice a year, depending on the amount of change in your customer's business.

Table 2.1 shows the objectives of a typical CVR.

Objectives of a Customer Value Review (CVR)

- Get Credit for the value you have delivered (**Past Value Delivered**, PVD).

- Share status and address any **open issues** in the Customer Success Plan.

- Uncover what is **changing and newly important** to the customer's business.

- Determine **who** these changes impact and create **compelling reasons to meet with them.**

- **Develop and start to qualify new sales pipeline opportunities to pursue (Value Creation).**

Table 2.1

Do not be intimidated by the breadth of these objectives. The size, scope, and complexity of your solutions and implementation should dictate the detail and complexity of your review. I've seen clients effectively accomplish these objectives with an email overview of the Customer Success

Plan followed by a brief conference call. In other instances, a brief, in-person meeting using the CSP slides was sufficient. Again, the size and importance of the outcomes you expect to deliver will dictate the best means of fulfilling the meeting objectives. One word of caution, though: mind your assumptions. If the deal you sold was not that large or important to you, don't assume it was not important to the customer. And if you sold to a smaller business, don't assume that your solution was less important to them than it might be to your larger customers. In my experience, smaller customers care just as much about their business outcomes as larger customers (sometimes more)—and every large business grew from a small one.

THE CVR MEETING

To kick off your CVR meeting, start by getting to the heart of the matter by presenting the value you believe you delivered to your customer. Do this by presenting to the key decision makers the mutual Scorecard with the results you believe have been delivered. This will allow them to validate the results. Do not present the results as a *fait accompli* or fact. Your opinion is not what counts here. You want the key decision maker(s) to be able to articulate and validate the value they believe they have received and then give you credit for it.

Now you have earned the right to ask your customer: What is important to you *today*? What is changing with your business? What other business challenges could we potentially help you address? Are there new opportunities we could help you capitalize on? When you make time after the sale and implementation to sit down and ensure you have delivered the promised value, your customer should be more than willing to open up and discuss their *current* issues. (See the sidebar for a real-life example.)

One of my clients delivered a solution that allowed their customer to extend the life of their existing IT infrastructure and thus support the enterprise another twenty to twenty-four months. (Note: this was introduced in The Irresistible Value Proposition.) There was no budget for the solution due to spending cuts across the board, so the sales team presented the following value proposition. "Your top priority is to continue to support business operations. Our software solution will reduce your current data storage volume by approximately 27 percent by removing all duplicate files in your data. This will extend the life of your current infrastructure by at least twenty to twenty-four months."

The overriding issue was a quick implementation as the existing infrastructure was going to run out of storage within several months. During the CVR, the key decision maker, a senior VP, readily acknowledged the terrific value the original deal (a seven-digit sole-source award) had delivered, and the remainder of the meeting concerned new issues and opportunities he was addressing and how my client might help. The result was an even larger, eight-digit sole-source deal that closed in less than four months! It's worth repeating that this additional business was with a customer that had slashed budgets because of declining sales. This is why you should make the CVR a regular part of your selling and account management motion!

In addition to getting credit for PVD, your goal is to be offered new opportunities by being *relevant* to your customer's key decision makers. You become relevant and more strategic by focusing on the things that are important to the business *and* personal success of the key decision makers. You must demonstrate that you will get in the boat and row with them to help them achieve their outcomes. This will build a fortress-like defense around your current business and open new opportunities to sell.

When you deliver value to the people who matter, you make it very hard for a competitor to steal that business. But that doesn't mean they won't try. Most contenders will come in with a "lower price" tactic designed to hook the customer's short-term thinking at the cost of more strategic outcomes. In the real-world sidebar example above, the senior VP needed to deliver results that were critical to the ongoing operations of the business. How likely would he have been to switch vendors and sacrifice an outcome critical to the future of his business for a potentially lower price?

More than once, I've seen key decision makers on the buying side take the CSP (at least the Scorecard and Implementation Plan) further up their organizations to get credit for the value *they* have delivered. I've seen a CIO take it to the CEO and CFO. I've also seen the CEO take it to the board. This accomplishes two things important to you: the decision makers get the credit (and presumably a dose of job security), and it increases the risk to the buying company of switching suppliers (not to mention the political implications to the key decision makers). The risk of switching suppliers is simply too high, and the combination of the credit gained by the stakeholders with the tangible switching cost to the business goes a long way toward making the seller "bullet proof" in the account. (See sidebar.)

I'm not a big fan of the tactic of "buying market share" by offering a much lower price—a common practice in B2B sales. How do I help my clients combat this when competitors try to steal their accounts? By ensuring that they deliver the promised value using Customer Success Plans and then get credit for delivering that value via Customer Value Reviews.

But what if one of my clients wants to steal market share by unseating an incumbent competitor? In that case, I recommend that they simply go in and ask the following: "You've committed a lot of funds and resources to XYZ Company. Can you share with me what value you have gotten from this investment?" If the prospect can't answer this question (which is almost always), my client has now set the stage for winning that business based on delivering real value, not on offering the lowest price. If the incumbent supplier didn't sell to outcomes important to the buyer (again, almost always) and then construct the "right deal" to deliver those outcomes, the best way to turn a toehold into a foothold—or maybe throw the door wide open—is to invite the buyer to talk about the value they wanted to receive that their current vendor failed to deliver.

Once you have solidified your position in an account, your next objective is to develop new sales pipeline. You want to uncover potential opportunities to create value for your customer and thus generate additional revenue for your company—and yourself. Congratulations! You've essentially completed a full "rotation" of the Value Lifecycle™, and you are back to the Create Value phase of a *new* cycle. Contrary to what you may have experienced in the past, selling is not a linear world, nor should it be transactional or tactical. The Value Lifecycle™ frames a strategic world, one with long-term success at stake.

CREATING VALUE—AGAIN

You've now arrived back where you began the *Must-Win Deals* series. This time, however, you understand the plot and have a proven script to follow moving forward with your new account. First, create the potential for value for your customer by gaining a mutual understanding of what they are trying to achieve this time around (outcomes) and how they will measure success (value). Don't be surprised if they freely share this information with you as you have been through the Value Lifecycle™ together—and they most likely want more of the same!

Then, through your value proposition, succinctly advise the customer what you intend to deliver this time and what they should expect from you. Again, present a compelling proposal that allows your customer to buy from you and structure the right deal for them. And again, they will expect you to present options so that they can make an informed decision and make it their deal.

Finally, negotiate a great deal that is good for both parties, which will increase the probability of once more delivering the promised value. After the sale (or even better, before the PO is issued), you should jointly develop a Customer Success Plan for delivering the value. Finally, execute on delivery and go back to the customer to "self-report" via a Customer Value Review. The CVR cannot be optional (especially in a subscription or recurring revenue business) because customer churn can quickly kill your business model, resulting in anemic Net Revenue Retention (NRR) growth that will decimate the market value of your business.[7]

It's truly unfortunate that from the perspective of most customers, it is uncommon for sellers to offer to "self-report" on their performance of delivering value—surprising too because the CVR is such a great way to powerfully

---

7   If it were up to me, CSPs and CVRs would be a condition of employment for any sales rep that reported to me. It's that important! *This* is how you can significantly address the issues of customer churn and not enough qualified sales pipeline.

and positively differentiate your company. How different would you look to your customers if this was the way you routinely did business?

Let's now see how a Customer Success Plan and Customer Value Review might be used to drive real business success by turning our attention back to the Case Story where Paul and the Agile team are developing their Customer Success Plan for the kickoff meeting with MFS.

CHAPTER 3

Case Story Conclusion

CAST OF CHARACTERS: RECAP

1. **Paul Stockard**, *Agile Sales Rep*: Paul is the Sales Rep for Agile Information Solutions (Agile). He has been calling on Worldwide Financial Solutions, Inc. (Worldwide) for the past five months and more recently Mega Financial Services (MFS) after the acquisition.

2. **Jane Jones**, *Agile Sales Engineer*: Jane handles all the technical aspects of an opportunity and manages proof-of-concept tests with a customer prior to a sale. She also supports the customer after the sale.

3. **Douglas Hand**, *Agile Lead Engineer for Services and Support*: Doug is responsible for implementation after the sale as well as customer support. He and his team will lead the integration project.

4. ***Jared Carlisle***, *Agile Sr. Financial Analyst*: Jared's job is to ensure that any Agile offering will be profitable to the company as well as in line with deals given to other customers. He also helps account teams quantify the value they expect to deliver to customers.

5. ***Caroline Borders***, *Agile VP of Legal*: Caroline is an experienced attorney who handles most legal negotiations of contracts, terms, and conditions with customers.

6. ***Tim Rosser***, *Agile VP of Sales*: Tim is an experienced IT sales executive who is known to be unflappable, as well as a great coach and mentor. Paul and his team have a very good relationship with Tim.

7. ***Susan Renly***, *Worldwide Chief Information Officer (CIO)*: Susan has been a long-time supporter of Agile and Paul. The recent acquisition of Worldwide by MFS has created a terrific career opportunity for her as she is in the running for the position of CIO of MFS. (The previous CIO recently left the company.) This would be a significant jump in responsibility and pay and now appears to be contingent on the successful integration of Worldwide into MFS.

8. ***Mike Sorenson***, *Worldwide VP of Technology*: Mike has been Susan's "right-hand man" and key to the success

of Worldwide. He will play a critical role in the successful integration of MFS, AIC, and Worldwide.

9. **Kenneth Beckley**, *Former CEO of Worldwide*: Kenneth is a supporter of the cloud-based approach used by Agile and has been named to the MFS Board of Directors as part of the acquisition. His first assignment is to ensure access to the Worldwide applications and data by the MFS salesforce.

10. **Bill Sellers**, *MFS SVP of Operations*: Bill heads up the steering committee and has been charged by the MFS Board of Directors with completing the Worldwide IT integration in less than four months. It appears he has been given significant incentives to do so as he is anxious to get the integration underway.

11. **Jack Grossman**, *MFS VP of Technology*: Also on the steering committee, Jack's role is to determine the integration approach. Jack is also in the running for the newly open MFS CIO position. He was a big supporter of JCN, the primary competition to Agile, so his support during the implementation is suspect.

12. **Stephanie Holder**, *MFS Sr. Procurement Manager*: MFS has a reputation as a very tough negotiator, and Stephanie is a big reason for that. It also appears that

the procurement department wields a lot of influence and power at MFS. She and Paul just finished negotiating the deal between Agile and MFS.

Just days before the start of formal negotiations between Paul Stockard and Stephanie Holder, JCN, one of Agile's arch-competitors, had offered a "hail Mary" proposal for a new cloud-based solution with an offer to waive the first year's fees and services. In their meeting, Stephanie tried to use this last-minute proposal as leverage in the negotiation with Agile, and in response, Tim Rosser abruptly and emphatically announced that she should take the JCN offer before it was rescinded, as Agile would not consider anything close to JCN's disruptive offer. Then, with an offer to pull Agile's proposal so that she could begin negotiations with JCN, Tim left the room—to the genuine shock of both Stephanie *and* Paul.

Stephanie briefly grilled Paul to be sure that Tim's theatrics were not a stunt, and once she was satisfied that Paul's surprise was real, the two of them decided to continue working together to see if they could reach an agreement. Paul then took a calculated risk and informed Stephanie of a recent demonstration of Worldwide's technology and client portal in a meeting attended by the MFS CEO, Bill Sellers and members of the board. That prompted Stephanie to call for a break, and when she returned (presumably now up to speed on the impact of the demonstration), she informed Paul that they should try and use the remainder of the day to reach an agreement that would work for MFS and Agile. After hours of tough give and take, Stephanie and Paul landed on a deal—one that contained the key deal levers that would increase the odds that they both could deliver the promised value within the board's aggressive timeline.

Stephanie then gave Agile permission to meet with anyone at MFS and Worldwide to complete a Customer Success Plan and prepare for the formal kickoff meeting the following Monday.

THE KICKOFF MEETING

Monday morning of the kickoff meeting found Paul wondering where the past week had gone. After closing the deal last Tuesday, the Agile account team and members of the MFS and Worldwide teams had worked nonstop through the remainder of the week and over the weekend finalizing the Customer Success Plan.

The first big change came on Wednesday, the day after the deal was struck, when Bill Sellers informed everyone that the Worldwide platform, portal, and interfaces would need to be rebranded as MFS. Apparently, the demonstration attended by Bill, the MFS CEO, and board members the previous Monday had made quite an impression. The MFS salesforce would also need to be trained on the newly rebranded platform.

Susan Renly stepped up and took charge of that task as she had the right person on her team to handle it: **Mike Sorenson**. Mike had been her "right-hand man" for several years, and he knew the Worldwide systems inside and out. He would be assisted by Jane Jones from Agile. Jane was also familiar with the Worldwide systems and had the technical skills to make the changes. A representative from MFS marketing would provide Jane and Mike with the current MFS marketing scheme. Susan also volunteered the current VP of Sales at Worldwide to put together and conduct the training of the MFS Salesforce.

With the first major change addressed, everything else about the implementation required detailed planning but was consistent with the pre-planning already started by the Agile team. Over the weekend, Bill Sellers stopped by to check on progress (and bring pizzas), which only reinforced to Paul and the Agile team how important these integrations were.

Monday's kickoff meeting would be run by Doug Hand of Agile and Susan Renly, with Doug managing Agile's efforts to integrate MFS and Worldwide and Susan overseeing the AIC integration. In attendance were Bill Sellers, Jack Grossman and his key direct reports, most of the Worldwide IT team that reported to Susan, the entire Agile Implementation Team assigned to MFS, as well as Tim Rosser and Paul. While Tim hadn't attended every negotiation (namely the ones he walked out on), he or another Agile executive would pointedly attend every kickoff meeting by way of reinforcing to each customer how important the delivery of value was to Agile.

Paul took a seat and surveyed the room, and he was surprised to see Stephanie Holder walk in. Catching his eye, she waved and smiled briefly, then walked over to Tim Rosser, shook his hand, and started what appeared to be an animated but friendly conversation before taking a seat in the back.

Wow, Paul thought. *She's acting friendly, and I'm surprised she decided to attend after all. I wish I could've heard her conversation with Tim.*

The meeting went extremely well as both Doug and Susan were well prepared and their teams knew what was expected of them. Bill Sellers was engaged and complimentary about the thoroughness of the Customer Success Plan. Paul was still amazed that the Agile, Worldwide, and MFS teams had been able to pull everything together on such a short timeline. The only group members who did not actively participate in the meeting were Jack Grossman and his direct reports.

Come to think of it, they weren't around to help out last weekend, Paul mused. Was that because the role of Jack and his team was just to "keep the lights on" during the integration? After all, this was something Jack had pointedly reminded everyone of during the first several days of planning. *Maybe it's just sour grapes.*

At the close of the kickoff meeting, Stephanie approached Paul. "Paul, by now I shouldn't be surprised," she said with a wry smile, "but that plan is complete and impressive. I really hope it works."

"Stephanie, thank you!" Paul said sincerely, shaking her hand. "That means a lot, coming from you. I hope you feel the same as we go through the implementation. There's plenty of work ahead, and we all know that a lot can change along the way!"

Tim Rosser was pleased with the meeting and the Customer Success Plan. After sharing his sincere thanks with the Agile Implementation team, he pulled Paul aside and whispered, "Keep an eye on Jack Grossman and his team. Something seems off here, and we don't need any more surprises."

Paul nodded his understanding and filed it away. Tim was known to be a shrewd judge of character, and soon enough, Jack proved him right. Two days after the kickoff meeting, Jack Grossman handed in his resignation along with three of his direct reports. For an already-under-staffed MFS IT team, this was a major blow. Now MFS lacked sufficient staff to operate the current infrastructure, much less support any integration efforts. Many assumed that Jack simply couldn't see how he would fit into a modern, cloud-based IT operation. And perhaps he was right. Whatever the reason, the timing of his departure, along with key members of his staff, needed to be dealt with—and quickly!

This prompted an emergency meeting with Paul Stockard, Bill Sellers, Susan Renly, Stephanie Holder, and Doug Hand. Susan quickly showed her leadership acumen by taking charge of the situation.

"I'd like to volunteer to take over the management of the current MFS IT operations," she began. "In my place, Mike Sorenson can assume day-to-day management of the AIC integration. He's done most of the planning and is well qualified to handle it."

"That sounds like a solid plan," Bill agreed. "But we also need to prioritize replacing the missing staff at MFS."

"I can bring on Agile IT Engineers to help fill the missing slots until replacements can be found," Paul offered.

Susan and Bill vigorously nodded their agreement, and Bill asked Stephanie to get with Paul and execute the change order as soon as possible. Because they had already negotiated service rates, this was a quick administrative task, and Agile's temporary engineers were on site at MFS the next day. Less of a quick fix would be hiring full-time replacement MFS IT personnel, but again, Susan volunteered to lead this effort.

"Guys, I think I have a good grasp of the long-term skills we'll need as MFS moves to a cloud-based operation," she said. "And I've got good contacts in the industry I won't hesitate to call for leads on candidates. I'd like to ask Jane

Jones to help me with that, as well as with the screening and interview process."

Susan surprised everyone in the meeting with that comment. But she trusted Jane's judgment and felt that Jane knew what was needed in a candidate. With Bill and Paul's agreement, they now had a plan. Barring any further surprises, they could now turn their attention to the main task at hand and the road ahead.

The ensuing integration and standardization on the Worldwide platform were as intense a six-week period as Paul had ever experienced. Though Paul had no direct role in the implementation (which was handled admirably by Susan, Doug, Jane, and Mike), he tried to make himself useful—even if that meant making coffee and doughnut runs. Along the way, there were a number of tough technical issues to resolve, but as the Agile team reminded Paul, most were issues they had expected and planned for.

Susan seemed to be everywhere at once throughout the implementation. She even tasked Paul with ensuring that daily and weekly meetings among the key staff at Agile, Worldwide, and MFS were held and fully attended and that all action items were followed up on.

THE CUSTOMER VALUE REVIEW

Six weeks later, Paul and Tim walked into MFS headquarters to conduct the first of what Paul hoped would be many Customer Value Reviews. With twenty minutes to kill before meeting with Bill Sellers and Susan Renly, they settled into chairs in the lobby, where Paul had time to reflect on a strange new feeling: the sensation of *not* being the least bit nervous about a meeting with MFS executives! His team had done such a fantastic job at MFS over the previous six weeks, there was little he could find to be concerned about.

As a result of the win, Paul had received the biggest commission check of his life, and he was going to club! What's more, Tim had shared confidentially that Paul's entire team would also be invited to club, which was highly unusual, and they had all just received sizable bonuses. However, as Paul's wife had reminded him, he had yet to take that promised vacation. *Maybe after this CVR is done*, he thought.

The new integrated platform had gone live a little over a week ago, and the market buzz followed quickly, touting the new MFS go-to-market strategy and offerings. Just yesterday, one industry journal trumpeted "the return of MFS" to its former prominence, highlighting the positive customer response to their new platform. Assets under management and customer count had both grown in just the first week of operation, and MFS's stock price was at a fifty-two-week high, up almost 15 percent from the low of two months ago. Paul felt justifiably proud of Agile's performance. At the same time, he was grateful to Susan for all her help and to Bill Sellers for his confidence in Agile. Now it was time to meet with them and self-report on the value he believed Agile had delivered.

Exiting the elevator, Paul and Tim narrowly dodged a dolly stacked with packing boxes being wheeled out of Bill's office. Neither Bill nor his EA were anywhere to be found, so the two simply looked at each other and shrugged, not knowing what to make of it. As they turned to head back to the receptionist in the lobby, a pleasant woman intercepted them and introduced herself as the executive assistant for **Arlisa Bennett**.

"Paul and Tim from Agile, right?" she asked. The men nodded yes. "I was told to look out for you. You're on the wrong floor if you're looking for Bill!" she said with a quick laugh. "His new office is one floor up. Just take a quick left off the elevator, and you'll see it in the corner. Have a great day!"

Paul and Tim followed her directions, and this time the elevator doors opened to a floor clearly meant to convey success and authority, although they still had to run a gauntlet of boxes and dollies on their way to the corner office. As they approached, they couldn't miss a new placard: Bill Sellers – Chief Operating Officer. Before Paul could process it all, Bill walked up, smiling broadly, and shook his hand.

"Pardon my dust," he chuckled. "And sorry for the confusion, but things are happening fast, and I didn't have time to reach you."

"Absolutely no problem—promotions are a messy business," Tim said dryly, shaking Bill's hand.

The three men laughed hard—as much for the moment as for the humor.

"Seriously, congratulations!" Tim followed. "And if this is a bad time to meet, we can certainly reschedule."

"Not at all," Bill insisted. "I didn't want to miss this meeting, so I had my assistant reserve a room."

As they walked to the conference room, Paul wondered where Susan Renly could be. It was not like her to miss a meeting—especially one that now included the COO of MFS!

Settling into comfortable chairs around a mahogany table, Paul pulled out the five-page CVR for Bill and a copy for Susan. He handed Bill his copy and said, "Bill, I assume Susan will be joining us. Should we wait for her before we start?"

Bill smiled, eyes twinkling. "No, Susan will be a bit delayed. Why don't we start, and you can fill her in later?"

Paul glanced at Tim, who looked a bit perplexed but simply nodded, and so they began.

MFS
MEGA FINANCIAL SYSTEMS

MFS Customer Success Plan:
Integrate the Worldwide and AIC
Acquisitions Ahead of Board Deadline

Paul Stockard – Account Manager
November 2, 2020

Ag*i*le

Figure 3.1

Agile liked to keep the CVR informal, which they found invited dialogue with the customer. It also helped that the CVR itself was only four pages (plus a cover). The one Bill was looking at now had been jointly developed by Agile, MFS, and Worldwide, in the same format presented at the kickoff meeting. It started with the Scorecard of all the agreed success metrics with current status and brief explanations where appropriate. A simple color code of red, yellow, and green provided a quick status check for each outcome. Both sides decided that only successfully completed items should be colored green. Yellow items were still in process, even if they were on schedule.

MFS Outcomes Scorecard — Ag*i*le

Focus Areas	Outcomes / Metrics	Value Delivered	Notes / Action Items
Worldwide / MFS Integration	Compile and Reformat MFS Account Data by 10/12/20	Completed 10/11/20 ahead of schedule	None
	Import MFS Account Data by 10/19/20	Completed 10/15/20 ahead of schedule	None
	Rebrand Worldwide Platform, Portal, and Interfaces to MFS by 10/23/20	Completed 10/20/20 ahead of schedule	None
	Train MFS Sales on Worldwide Platform, Portal, and Interfaces by 10/24/20	Completed 10/23/20 on schedule	None
	MFS IT Manage Agile Platform by 11/2/20	Scheduled for 11/30/20 - Delayed	Hire for IT Staff Turnover
	Go Live (100% Uptime) by 10/26/20	Platform Live on 10/23/20 (100% Uptime)	None
AIC Integration	Compile and Reformat AIC Account Data by 11/2/20	Completed 10/28/20 ahead of schedule	None
	Import AIC Account Data by 11/9/20	Ahead of schedule for Import on 11/5/20	Daily Tracking
	Complete "Hot Updates" – Zero Downtime	2 Hot Updates 10/28/20 (100% Uptime)	Included Platform Upgrade
	AIC Go Live on MFS by 11/9/20	Ahead of schedule for Go Live on 11/5/20	Daily Tracking

Figure 3.2

Bill glanced through the Scorecard[8] and paused at several items concerning the AIC integration to ask some clarifying questions. This was not the first time he had seen the data, as it had been continually available to him and Susan Renly. He then spent a few minutes on the only red item, the hiring of MFS replacement IT staff. Paul never liked presenting a red item on any CVR, but everyone in the room knew that this issue did not reflect negatively on Agile's performance.

In fact, Bill commented, "I want to thank you both—and especially Jane Jones—for all your support in helping us address the staff turnover issue. I'll confess that I was really concerned about this early on, but with the terrific people you brought in to augment the staff and the work Susan and Jane have done on hiring, it's been handled well."

"Bill, thank you," Paul said. "We were glad to provide that help, especially knowing that our people would get the job done. As for today, we know the major impetus behind this initiative was to get the MFS and Worldwide integration done ahead of the board's deadline. Now that you've been live for about a week, is there any feedback you can give us?"

8   In the Value Delivered column, red items are colored black, yellow items light gray, and green items medium gray.

Bill smiled as he looked from Paul to Tim. "This is confidential, but I got a text over the weekend from the CFO stating that last week's sales figures were almost 15 percent above the prior week. And he's very happy with the new product mix of those sales. On top of that, he's taken more calls from stock analysts the past few days than in the past few months. Now, of course, he's wanting the AIC integration completed as soon as possible as he thinks that will drive another big sales jump!"

"As you can surmise," Bill continued, "increasing revenues, improving the quality of those revenues, and eventually bumping the stock price were the reasons we undertook this acquisition. Right now, the executive team at MFS is looking really smart, in no small part due to your efforts.

"So, what *other* good news do you have for me?" Bill concluded with a chuckle.

Paul turned to the Implementation Plan. "We are actually ahead of schedule, or more precisely, Susan and Mike have us ahead of schedule for the AIC integration. We could potentially move up the go-live date to the fifth if that works for you and the CFO."

I just wish Susan were here to get the credit she truly deserves, Paul thought.

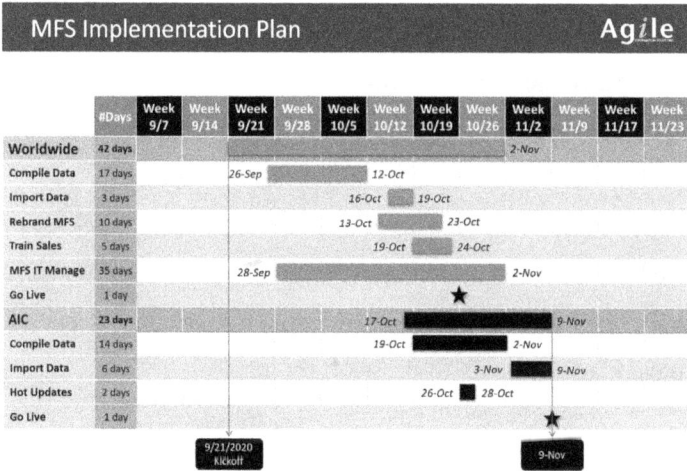

	#Days	Week 9/7	Week 9/14	Week 9/21	Week 9/28	Week 10/5	Week 10/12	Week 10/19	Week 10/26	Week 11/2	Week 11/9	Week 11/17	Week 11/23
Worldwide	42 days									2-Nov			
Compile Data	17 days			26-Sep			12-Oct						
Import Data	3 days						16-Oct	19-Oct					
Rebrand MFS	10 days					13-Oct		23-Oct					
Train Sales	5 days						19-Oct	24-Oct					
MFS IT Manage	35 days			28-Sep						2-Nov			
Go Live	1 day							★					
AIC	23 days						17-Oct				9-Nov		
Compile Data	14 days						19-Oct		2-Nov				
Import Data	6 days									3-Nov	9-Nov		
Hot Updates	2 days							26-Oct	28-Oct				
Go Live	1 day										★		

MFS Implementation Plan — Ag*i*le

9/21/2020 Kickoff   9-Nov

Figure 3.3

Bill smiled and said, "Susan and Mike have done a terrific job handling this, and I wish we could move up the go-live date, at least to keep the CFO happy, but we need to keep it on the ninth because that's the date we've given AIC customers for their current online portal to cut over to the new MFS portal." He briefly looked over the Implementation Plan, then added, "Susan and I are hopeful we'll have all the staffing and training done by the end of the month, but if not, I want you and Stephanie to be ready to extend the staff augmentation and training schedule for another two to four weeks as a back-up plan."

Paul agreed and said he would get the paperwork ready for Stephanie, just in case.

Bill then furrowed his brow at Paul and Tim in mock consternation. "And speaking of Stephanie, I don't know what happened during your negotiations, but you two seem to have made quite an impression on her."

Tim smiled. "I hope we demonstrated to her that our goal is to always do a great deal that is good for you as well as us."

"Well, you certainly don't have to sell *me* on that!" Bill laughed. "But she told me the other day she is enjoying working with Agile, and especially you, Paul."

"Stephanie was a tough customer and a serious negotiator," Paul responded. "I just don't think she'd ever been up against a supplier who was just as interested in *delivering* value as she was in *getting* it!"

He continued, "If everybody's ready, let's talk about Changes and Innovations."

Changes and Innovations			Ag*i*le

Focus Areas	Change / Innovation	Responsible (Agile & MFS)	Action Items
Changes	Staff Attrition of MFS IT Engineers	D. Hand / S. Renly	Reschedule Platform Training – **DONE**
	Agile Engineers Staff Augmentation Support for MFS IT	P. Stockard / S. Holder	Through 11/30/20 – **DONE**
	Hiring of MFS IT Engineers	J. Jones / S. Renly	8 of 10 Hired – **IN PROCESS**
	Extend Platform Training Scope	P. Stockard / S. Holder	Extend through 11/30/20 – **DONE**
Innovations	Dataccess Cloud Platform Update Version 13.18.25 Available 10/15/18	D. Hand / S. Renly, M. Sorenson	Schedule Dataccess Platform Upgrade – **DONE**
	Updated Integration Scoping Process	D. Hand / M. Sorenson	Train MFS IT Staff and Implement on AIC – **DONE**
	Re-Platforming Process Update / Revision	D. Hand / M. Sorenson	Testing on AIC Integration – **IN PROCESS**

Figure 3.4

Scanning the section, Bill said, "Doug and Mike told me last week they had some thoughts to improve the re-platforming and integration processes based on what they learned doing the Worldwide integration. Have you seen their planned improvements?"

"Yes, we have," Tim responded, "and I'm pretty excited about it as it may change some of the things we routinely do for *all* future Agile customers. These have the potential to give us an even bigger competitive advantage in the market."

Bill was glad to hear that; he always wanted valued suppliers to become even more successful. Apparently satisfied, he looked at both Paul and Tim and said, "To say I am pleased with your performance would be an understatement! As far as I'm concerned, Agile has done everything you promised and then some, and I'm glad to be able to tell you this personally. To say the least, you'll have no problem getting the good references you wanted from MFS."

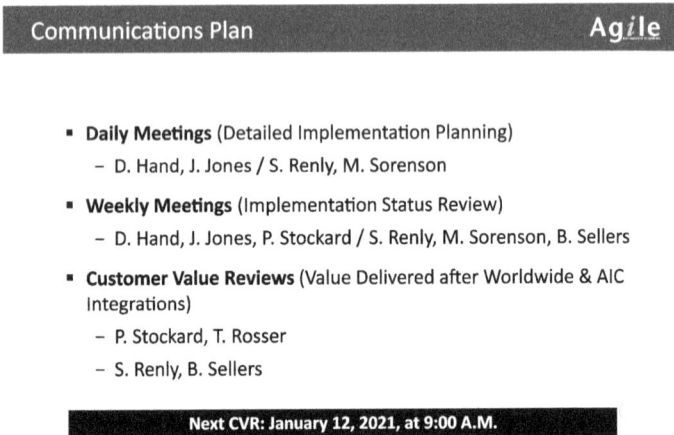

Communications Plan	Ag*i*le

- **Daily Meetings** (Detailed Implementation Planning)
  - D. Hand, J. Jones / S. Renly, M. Sorenson
- **Weekly Meetings** (Implementation Status Review)
  - D. Hand, J. Jones, P. Stockard / S. Renly, M. Sorenson, B. Sellers
- **Customer Value Reviews** (Value Delivered after Worldwide & AIC Integrations)
  - P. Stockard, T. Rosser
  - S. Renly, B. Sellers

Next CVR: January 12, 2021, at 9:00 A.M.

Figure 3.5

"However," Bill continued in a somewhat more restrained voice, "because of my new position, I'm afraid I won't take part in any future value reviews with you. Next week, I'll set up a meeting with my replacement, Arlisa Bennett, so you all can get to know her. I'll also give her my copy of the Customer Success Plan and brief her on the details. Arlisa reports directly to me, and I'll make sure she keeps me apprised of your progress. And I certainly expect you to have more work here at MFS! Any questions?"

Paul and Tim looked at each other, and as Paul was about to speak, there was a brief knock at the door. When it opened, there stood Susan Renly, looking very happy if a bit tired. She began to apologize, but Bill cut her off, announcing, "Gentlemen, I am thrilled to introduce the new CIO of MFS!" The room broke out into applause, and there were congratulations and handshakes all around. Approaching Paul, Susan dispensed with formalities and gave him a big hug.

"Susan, I couldn't be happier for you," Paul exclaimed. "No one deserves this more!"

Bill then excused himself when his EA poked her head in the door.

Susan closed the door behind Bill, then turned to Tim and Paul and said with a smile, "Let's take a seat, but we can dispense with the formal CVR as I know exactly what the metrics say—and they're all great! Instead, I want to talk about how Agile can help me turn MFS into an acquisition machine…"

THE END…OF THE BEGINNING

They say we are a species that learns best through stories. My goal in creating the "Case Story" that ties this series together was to provide an informative and (hopefully) entertaining way to show how the key concepts of the Value Lifecycle™ fit together throughout a sales campaign and then after the sale. My hope is that Paul and Susan's journey—with the rest of the "cast and crew"—through a complex sale animates these concepts in a way that makes them more memorable and therefore more practical.

Any similarity to actual companies and/or individuals is purely coincidental, of course, although I can say that the scenarios and character types were drawn from my firsthand experience in sales, as a sales executive, and more importantly the work I have had the privilege of doing with both selling and buying clients. I have probably learned more from these people than I ever imparted, and I am grateful for the opportunity to try to pass some of that learning along to you!

Finally, as for any "technology" depicted in the Case Story, I hope you won't take me to task on any issues of accuracy or functionality. I purposely kept the tech broad and vague as it was not intended to be the centerpiece—nor should it be for you "in real life," as the purpose of technology is to enable better and faster outcomes. Rather, I wanted to show how we can better sell in a highly competitive and ever-changing market where outcome-based value selling, proposing, negotiating, and account management can make you, the salesperson, the real differentiator. To that end, I hope you got value from this work of fiction!

CHAPTER 4

You're Almost Full Circle

Now, Keep It Going!

By now, I hope you have surmised that the heart of the Value Lifecycle™ model is driving and managing *value* for both the buyer and the seller. In this model, value is the keystone of the relationship between you and your customer. As the single point of reference for every opportunity you may pursue with your customer—both today and as you navigate change in the future—staying focused on value will ensure that the relationship you create is both durable and mutually profitable.

The strongest and most resilient B2B relationships form around value—especially *after* that value has been delivered. Customers don't need more relationships, even if those relationships are well managed. What they need is better ones, built around value provided by suppliers who will get in the boat and row with them to that distant shore called "success."

As I've argued throughout this series of books, your customers are not in the business of buying. They are in the business of *their business*. Making an informed buying decision in an ever-changing marketplace is simply not—nor will it ever be—in their wheelhouse. Therefore, the real issue you are addressing is that it is hard for your customers to make an informed buying decision. To bring this into sharper focus, Mediafly found that B2B buyer studies by Gartner, Forrester, and Challenger showed bona fide (approved) buying initiatives result in no award and no decisions *38–43 percent of the time.*[9] (Your biggest competitor, it turns out, is doing nothing!) Keeping value at the heart of your approach makes your customer's buying process easier by cutting through the fog of TMI (too much information), conflicting information, complexity, and uncertainty. This makes it easier for your customers to both *sell* internally on your behalf and *buy* from you.

Figure 4.1 summarizes the journey we've been on and the key questions we've been attempting to answer throughout the *Must-Win Deals* series of books.

9   Mediafly, "100+ Metrics that Matter for Sales Enablement, Content Marketing and Value Selling," https://www.mediafly.com/evolved-selling-community/metrics-matter.

THE VALUE LIFECYCLE™ IN ONGOING BUSINESS RELATIONSHIPS
Outcome-Based Value Propositions, Proposals, Great Deals, and PVD

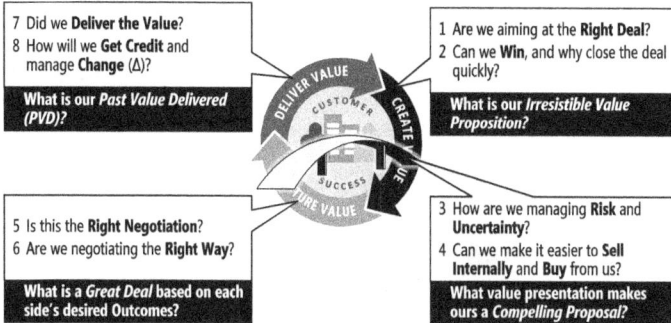

7 Did we **Deliver the Value**?
8 How will we **Get Credit** and manage **Change** (Δ)?

What is our *Past Value Delivered (PVD)*?

1 Are we aiming at the **Right Deal**?
2 Can we **Win**, and why close the deal quickly?

What is our *Irresistible Value Proposition*?

5 Is this the **Right Negotiation**?
6 Are we negotiating the **Right Way**?

What is a *Great Deal* based on each side's desired Outcomes?

3 How are we managing **Risk** and **Uncertainty**?
4 Can we make it easier to **Sell Internally** and **Buy** from us?

What value presentation makes ours a *Compelling Proposal*?

Figure 4.1

As I wrote at the beginning of our journey in *Must-Win Deals*, the Value Lifecycle™ is not a sales process, nor is it intended to take the place of one. Rather, it should help you *supercharge* your current sales, proposal, negotiation, and account management processes by focusing on the key outputs that are most important and impactful to the customer. In this series of books, I have structured books two through five to follow the Value Lifecycle™ model and along the way address the eight high-level, outcome-based value questions in Figure 4.1 above. The objective of each of these questions for a given phase is to produce the critical customer-facing outputs (black boxes) that will make it easier for the customer to buy, thus advancing the sale as quickly as possible, and then make it easier to stay with you and buy more.

Let's quickly summarize each phase of the Value Lifecycle™ along with its key outputs, listed here by **Phase** and *associated book*.

PHASE 1: CREATE VALUE—
THE IRRESISTIBLE VALUE PROPOSITION

Regardless of your current sales process, you should be able to answer the question, "Are we aiming at the right deal?" After all, if you are trying to sell the wrong deal for your customer and their specific situation, your odds of closing the deal will be extremely low. To determine the right deal, first discover the desired outcomes your customer wants to achieve (what they are buying) and then translate those outcomes into the key deal levers of your offer (what they are paying for).

Now, ask the two-part question, "Can we win, and why close the deal quickly?" As you've learned, you should win *only if* you can put more value on the table than the customer's most likely alternative (a competitor, doing nothing, or doing it themselves). If you cannot, you should consider exiting the sale or significantly changing the game and altering the customer's decision criteria. You want these criteria to be outcome-focused (especially outcomes you are uniquely positioned to deliver) versus feature- and function-based. Your customer should want to close a deal quickly because they see significant potential value for them.

Value is always incremental to the customer's alternative; therefore, your (differential) value must be readily recognized by the customer. As such, the key customer facing output at this phase is an Irresistible Value Proposition—one that gets your customer excited about doing business with you right now. If you can't get your customer excited about the prospect of doing business with you, your odds of winning will plummet, and your sales cycle will likely devolve into little more than a lengthy bidding war dressed up as a "negotiation"—what I term a "feature, function, price beauty contest."

PHASE 2: COMMUNICATE VALUE—
THE COMPELLING PROPOSAL

Your key customer-facing output at this phase is a Compelling Proposal, one that should serve as a bridge between selling (creating value) and the negotiation (capturing value).

Recognizing that every sale is fraught with uncertainty and risk, begin spanning that bridge by asking, "How are we managing risk and uncertainty?" What is creating risk to closing your deal? What are you uncertain about? You realize that you will never have perfect information, coming as it does from the customer and various buying influencers, some of whom you will never even meet. What's more, everyone will have their own agenda and won't necessarily be fully aligned on the outcomes they want to achieve. Yet, you are only closing one deal with this customer, not multiple deals with various customer stakeholders. Presenting multiple acceptable options as part of your proposal is how you will manage risk and uncertainty. Makes you wonder why anyone in sales would present one offer and then hope and pray it carries the day.

Now, ask, "Can we make it easier to sell internally and buy from us?" The answer here, of course, is to design your proposal to achieve specific objectives that are different from traditional "proposal" objectives. The objectives of your Compelling Proposal are to

1. Reinforce trust

2. Set up the right negotiation

3. Establish credibility

4. Manage uncertainty

5. Make it easy for the customer to both buy from you and sell internally

At the heart of your Compelling Proposal are multiple acceptable options (MAOs), which invite the customer to help craft the best deal for them. In this way, MAOs enable your customer to make the deal "their deal," one they will be confident about selling internally and highly motivated to close quickly. Done thoughtfully, MAOs manage the uncertainty and risk in the deal, thus significantly shortening sales cycles and taking a lot of the pain out of negotiations.

PHASE 3: CAPTURE VALUE—
THE PAINLESS NEGOTIATION

If you detect a bit of hyperbole in the title of the third book, you're not wrong, but it's there to draw your attention to an important point: nowhere is it engraved that all negotiations must be painful or contentious! When you ask, "Is this the right negotiation?" you are really asking if the negotiation has been effectively anchored on the customer's desired outcomes. If you have positioned and proposed effectively, then you have been successfully anchoring the negotiation from the very beginning. This is what it really means to be "negotiating all the time"!

You should also ensure that your *internal* negotiations have prepared you to squarely aim at a *great deal* with the full support of your internal stakeholders, armed with key deal levers that will empower you to deliver the promised value without having to fly back to the "mother ship" for approval of every proposed change. Start your internal negotiations early so that you will be prepared to negotiate with your customer by prioritizing and assigning limits (ask for – accept) for each deal lever. This will inoculate you against a host of procurement tactics, especially getting you to negotiate against yourself.

Now, ask, "Are we negotiating the right way?" The *right way* ensures that the negotiation is never anchored on a single issue or deal lever, that the conversation is about your customer's outcomes, and that you never concede on any deal lever. Rather, you will either *trade* for deal levers you want or trade deal levers *out of the deal*. This is how you keep the hard-earned value in the deal. Additionally, never agree that anything is settled and "off the table" until *everything* is agreed to. Negotiating this way signals to your customer that real value was in your initial offer(s) and that you are only prepared to change that offer at the cost of something in return, something that may affect their desired outcomes. Negotiating the *right way*—always respectfully and collaboratively—motivates the other side to want to get the deal done quickly and move on.

But remember, you're not just aiming at any deal, you want to close a *great deal*, which is the key customer-facing output of this phase. A great deal is good for you as it supports your selling objectives and advances your business strategy. It is good for your customer as it supports their buying objectives. Finally, a great deal must have the right deal levers, which will increase the odds that you can both ultimately deliver the promised value.

PHASE 4: DELIVER (AND GET CREDIT FOR) VALUE—*CAN'T-LOSE ACCOUNTS*

Remember, your goal is not to just win a deal but to win a long-term customer, one who will renew readily and proactively bring new opportunities for you to grow the relationship. But for this to happen you must ask, "Did we deliver the value?" The first step in delivering value is to sit down with your customer and jointly develop a Customer

Success Plan that will serve as the basis for the formal kickoff meeting. The CSP will include:

1. A Scorecard to track progress of value delivered

2. An Implementation Plan to detail how you will deliver on the promised outcomes

3. A process for capturing and managing innovations and changes throughout the implementation

4. A Communications Plan to establish who should be meeting to track and manage progress, and how often

The key customer facing output at this phase is a clear tally of Past Value Delivered (PVD). But the CSP alone does not ensure that value delivery is perceived by the customer. After the sale, you must also ask, "How will we get credit and manage change?" Credit for PVD will be critical to your ongoing success at any account. Key decision makers on the buying side use PVD to get credit and accolades for the value *they* have brought their business. Your PVD also makes it much easier for them to justify renewals and support buying additional products and services from you. You build credit by conducting Customer Value Reviews on a regular basis with key decision makers, with two objectives. First, you want to receive credit for PVD and ensure renewals. Second, and importantly, you want to uncover any changes that are affecting your customer's business (signified by the Greek letter delta: Δ) and determine whether these changes could generate new opportunities for you.

You have now come full circle, and you are back at the beginning of the Value Lifecycle™, ready to create the potential for value. Here, it may be worth calling back to the source of the four key customer-facing outputs of the Value Lifecycle™ as first introduced in *Must-Win Deals*. (See Figure 4.2.)

CHALLENGES TO CLOSING MUST-WIN DEALS
Key Challenges from the Customer's Perspective

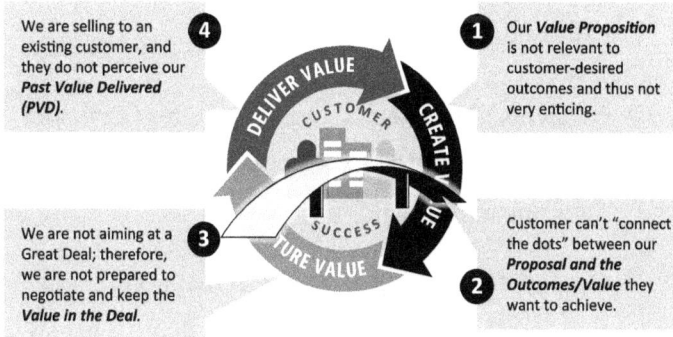

We are selling to an existing customer, and they do not perceive our *Past Value Delivered (PVD)*. ④

Our *Value Proposition* is not relevant to customer-desired outcomes and thus not very enticing. ①

We are not aiming at a Great Deal; therefore, we are not prepared to negotiate and keep the *Value in the Deal*. ③

Customer can't "connect the dots" between our *Proposal and the Outcomes/Value* they want to achieve. ②

Figure 4.2

Each output addresses the four key challenges sellers routinely present to buyers.

→ **Challenge:** Your value proposition is not relevant to customer-desired outcomes and thus not very enticing.

Output: An Irresistible Value Proposition that gets the customer excited about doing business with you.

→ **Challenge:** Your customer can't "connect the dots" between your proposal and the outcomes/value they want to achieve.

Output: A Compelling Proposal that makes those connections and thus makes it easier to sell internally and buy from you.

→ **Challenge:** You are not aiming at a great deal, and therefore, are not prepared to negotiate and keep the value in the deal.

Output: Negotiating a *great deal* that is good for both parties and increases the odds that the promised value will get delivered.

→ **Challenge:** You are selling to an existing customer, and they do not perceive your Past Value Delivered (PVD).

Output: Delivering and receiving credit for Past Value Delivered so that the customer wants to continue doing business with you.

There you have it. The more skillfully and proactively you tackle these four challenges over time, the more you should see increased conversion rates, shortened sales cycles, less discounting and higher-quality deals, reduced customer churn, and increased sales pipeline from upselling and cross-selling with current customers.

While this certainly begins to address the critical challenges facing sales organizations, I must confess there's one more challenge I've avoided discussing. It's arguably the biggest issue my clients struggle with, so let's dive in and see how the Value Lifecycle™ can help.

CHAPTER 5

Question "0"

Why Engage with You?

Let's start with a bit of a thought experiment. If I were to ask you how your opportunities are named and labeled in your CRM system, how would you answer? I'm willing to bet they are by customer name and product/service. The obvious next question is, "How do you talk about a given opportunity within your business?" My guess is, you talk about the "XYZ Company" and the "ABC Product" opportunity.

With that in mind, how compelling and interesting is that conversation likely to be to "XYZ Company"—or any customer? What about the key decision makers, who couldn't care less about the functional minutiae of your products—much less what clever name you use for them?

Bottom line: the way you talk about opportunities *inside your company* will directly impact the way you discuss them *when you are with customers*. (See sidebar.)

I had a client who recognized this issue and was determined to do something about it. Their solution was to go into the CRM system and strip out the name of every opportunity. The following guidelines were then given to each account team: one, no products or services will be in the name of the opportunity; and two, each opportunity must be named as the outcome(s) the account team is trying to help the customer achieve. This proved quite disruptive and challenging for most of the account teams—at least initially.

But the account teams eventually adjusted to the new system and began to discuss the opportunity to "help XYZ company reduce their time to market" or "improve customer retention by 5 percent," etc. Naturally, the way they talked about opportunities internally carried over to their customer-facing conversations. The impact was huge and helped them produce remarkable sales results. While this solution may not be for every company (it took a lot of senior management commitment and courage to see it through), it's a great example of the power of shifting from a product-centered selling mentality to one that is customer-outcome centered.

If you begin your selling motion discussing your "ABC Product," you're simply telling the customer it's really about the sale you want to make rather than the outcomes they want to achieve. You shouldn't be surprised then when the negotiation is just about price. And what about Past Value Delivered? How can you demonstrate meaningful PVD if it's just a function of what the customer paid for?

We all know how this ends. The real question is, "How did it even begin?" How did you get in front of the customer in the first place? The hard truth is that you may have gotten in front of someone in the buying organization, but you most likely *didn't* gain access to the key decision makers—a critical, missed opportunity you never knew about until it was too late.

QUESTION "0"

Before we get the chance to execute on the concepts described in the *Must-Win Deals* series, we first must gain access to prospects. This is the largest issue sales organizations struggle with today. It may be tempting to point the finger at marketing here, but not so fast—there are two different situations at play here. The first is selling to a current customer, and the second is getting in the door of a new prospect.

Let's start with existing customers, as our journey through the Value Lifecycle™ has already given us the tools we need here.

Figure 5.1 highlights where "Question 0" is in the Value Lifecycle™.

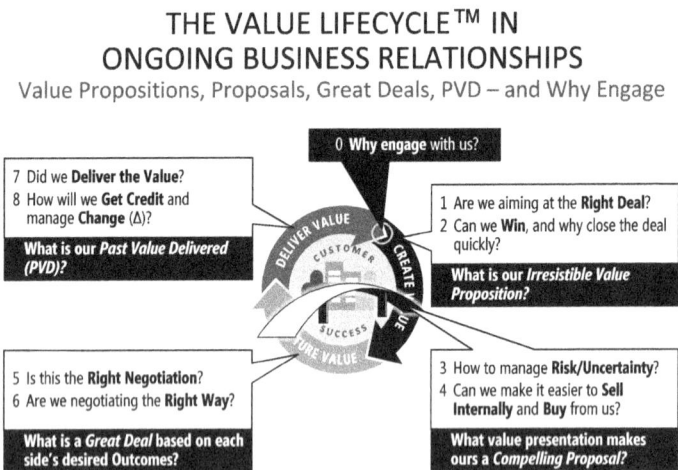

THE VALUE LIFECYCLE™ IN
ONGOING BUSINESS RELATIONSHIPS
Value Propositions, Proposals, Great Deals, PVD – and Why Engage

0 **Why engage** with us?

7 Did we **Deliver the Value**?
8 How will we **Get Credit** and manage **Change** (Δ)?

What is our *Past Value Delivered (PVD)*?

1 Are we aiming at the **Right Deal**?
2 Can we **Win**, and why close the deal quickly?

What is our *Irresistible Value Proposition*?

5 Is this the **Right Negotiation**?
6 Are we negotiating the **Right Way**?

What is a *Great Deal* based on each side's desired Outcomes?

3 How to manage **Risk/Uncertainty**?
4 Can we make it easier to **Sell Internally** and **Buy** from us?

What value presentation makes ours a *Compelling Proposal*?

Figure 5.1

"Question 0"—"Why engage with us?"—marks the beginning of the Create Value phase. For an existing customer, assuming you have delivered the value and received credit from previous purchases, answering this question should be as simple as falling off a log.

But how do you get in front of a *new* prospect? It stands to reason that if prospective customers are looking to *buy* new and improved outcomes, that's what they would be most interested in talking about. Yet, most B2B marketing messages are heavily product- and feature-focused, the stuff you *sell*—and what salespeople are incessantly trained on.

But key decision makers for prospective customers are much too busy to meet with you to talk about *your* company and *your* products. You're much more likely to meet with lower-level people charged with implementing and managing projects. As a result, their interest in you will be at the project level or because of a "cool" new feature or some tactical advantage your product may offer (at the right price, of course). Importantly, though, these lower-level people, tactical or not, are fully empowered to deliver a definitive "no," while any "yes" will be highly qualified and dependent on upstream approval (their internal selling skills) and the gauntlet of the purchasing process.

Even worse, these potential lower-level buyers likely have no interest in taking you to the key decision makers. That option has been foreclosed on by previous fearless sales reps who somehow managed to get in front of those decision makers only to do a "show up and throw up" presentation about their company, products, and services. Afterward, unknown to the sales rep, the lower-level champion was firmly advised to never let that happen again. (Does this sound familiar?)

At this point, if you're thinking that simply selling "harder" might solve the problem, think again. You need to be armed with something different, something that allows you to approach customers in a different way. More of the same thing here is the "definition of insanity," but unfortunately, this is the situation I find most of my clients in when I first engage with them. Here's the first step in breaking this vicious cycle.

POTENTIAL VALUE STATEMENT

Think of it this way: In today's competitive selling environment, a solid strategy, great products, and great services are simply "table stakes." By themselves, these things no longer provide a competitive advantage. Customers will buy from you because they derive *value* from doing business with you. Where in the past it may have been sufficient to be well versed on your company's products and services, with a solid portfolio of chiefly price-based selling tactics, today you need a Potential Value Statement (PVS), a document that provides a value-based foundation for your marketing messaging as well as your outreach programs (emails, cold call scripts, etc.).

The PVS is a simple, one-page *internal* document comprising the following sections:

→ One or two short sentences about **what** you do

→ One or two short paragraphs that describe **who** (key decision makers) typically engages your firm, their current business issues, and desired **outcomes**

→ Three to five short examples of **Past Value Delivered** from other customers who support your ability to deliver those outcomes

→ One to two *very brief* paragraphs about **how** your products/services *uniquely* deliver these outcomes to customers

Use the Potential Value Statement to internalize the right messaging to get in front of the key people at a prospect. Note the flow of the PVS. First, communicate what you do to provide context for your message. Next, offer examples of the types of individuals you have done business with.

(Select individuals with the same or similar titles to your current prospect.) Include their challenges, business issues, and the desired outcomes they wanted to achieve. This will give the prospect meaningful context for the potential value you might be able to deliver.

Next, provide real-world examples of Past Value Delivered, if possible, to *existing* customers. Showing that you are committed to delivering valuable business outcomes to past (or existing) customers will do more to boost your credibility than any other messaging. Only after setting this critical context do you get to talk about your products and services, and then only as a means for delivering *differentiated* value that helps your customers achieve their desired outcomes.

Have you noticed something familiar about the structure of the Potential Value Statement? It is framed and flows in the same basic phases as the Value Lifecycle™. However, it is framed and flows in the *opposite* order to typical product marketing messaging and product training! This is one of the reasons it is so challenging to develop these with clients. It takes the opposite (outside in) view than most are used to.

To develop a PVS, I typically involve several experienced sales reps, product marketing, support, and customer success people. It is especially difficult to distill this to one page, usually requiring three or four iterations. But the exercise is almost as important as the outcome, as you need to train yourself to get out of the weeds when discussing your potential value with prospective customers. After all, they only want to hear about what they're potentially *paying for* (your products and/or services) after you've convinced them you are focused squarely on what they are *buying* (better outcomes for their business), which you are uniquely qualified to deliver.

Think about it. If every customer-facing individual in your organization can't clearly articulate what you do, who reaches out to you and why, and the past value you've delivered to your customers, what will they end up talking about? You guessed it: your products and services. Below is an example of a Potential Value Statement.

POTENTIAL VALUE STATEMENT EXAMPLE

What We Do

We develop and deliver custom business apps into production quickly. These apps are hosted on a highly reliable and scalable cloud-based platform.

Who Engages Us

Senior business executives turn to us when they are frustrated by the time it takes to design, develop, and deploy business-critical applications. They are also plagued by unacceptable downtime and the inability to scale, causing negative impacts on their business and their customers. These executives are committed to developing highly effective and reliable apps in a short timeframe to keep pace with the speed of their business.

Proof Points

- **Increased Sales:** Automotive Company deployed thirty-plus applications into production in less than one year, increasing sales 17 percent to the targeted demographic.

- **Increased Shopping Basket:** Major Retail Store launched new applications weekly using 600 trained developers, increasing average shopping basket by 14 percent.

- **Increased Enterprise Accounts:** Major Telecom developed twelve business critical applications in production in less than six months, resulting in three large new enterprise customers.

- **Increased Customer Satisfaction:** SaaS firm experienced zero downtime in the first year and customer satisfaction improved 43 percent in three months.

- **Reduced Time to Market:** Financial Service Firm now deploys 80 percent faster with a 90 percent improvement in scaling factors, reducing their time to market by four months.

How We Uniquely Do This

We pioneered agile software development and processes to quickly scale application development. As a result, we can develop apps 75–100 percent faster, and we are constantly refining and improving our development processes.

Our platform was designed as cloud-native, making it much easier to develop and host applications. The platform is flexible and can easily integrate with any existing technology stack (on-premise or cloud) through APIs. Being cloud-based, it provides fast, nearly infinite scalability and is highly reliable with a 99.999 percent availability.

By far, the hardest part of developing the Potential Value Statement is capturing Past Value Delivered that is meaningful. *All* my clients can tell you who their customers are and what products and services they bought. *Some* can answer when asked how their customers use those products and services to run their business. *Very few* can answer when I ask, "So, what?" That is, what outcomes and *value* did this customer get from their products and services?

But outcomes are what your prospects are looking to *buy* from you, and the value they perceive is directly attached to those outcomes. The PVS is basically toothless without this information and becomes yet another discussion of your business, products, and services—the "same old" information that will never get you in front of the key decision makers.

Ideally, Past Value Delivered data comes from regular and recent Customer Value Reviews, which brings up a key point. The PVS is never "finished," and it should evolve as you uncover new use cases, new ways your customers use your products and services, business outcomes you can directly tie to your value, and ever-crisper ways of articulating that value. All of this will help you to optimize your value messaging for the prospect you are in front of.

The flow of the Potential Value Statement can also be a template for developing more targeted and interesting websites, more engaging marketing materials, sales collateral that actually *sells* when prospects read it, and outbound call scripts that are much more effective at generating fruitful leads. With a solid—and evolving—PVS in place, your *entry* point to the Value Lifecycle™ with new prospects should come to more closely resemble your re-entry point with existing customers!

* * *

By answering Question "0"—"Why engage with us?"—we have now truly come full circle, and I sincerely hope you have derived real value from our journey around the Value Lifecycle™. However, there's still work to be done. Making *meaningful changes* to how your organization manages value throughout the customer lifecycle will be challenging. There are almost no exceptions here. It is one thing to embrace a conceptual framework for putting value (to the customer) at the center of your selling process; it can be an entirely novel challenge, on the other hand, to begin to affect the changes in your company that will make the principles in the Value Lifecycle™ "second nature." It starts with ensuring that the questions you should be asking when you are in front of the customer are directly tied to the questions that everyone inside the selling organization is asking as well. And it will take time, effort, and practice to embed this new way of thinking.

If you are an executive or sales manager and you'd like to start implementing the concepts detailed throughout this series, I have created a series of "Questions for Changing the Conversation" in the Appendix. These are key questions that must be asked when conducting opportunity reviews, proposal/negotiation reviews, and account reviews. I have developed them over twenty years on thousands of B2B deals and have found that they work, regardless of industry or where you are in the world. If you are genuinely interested in flipping the script internally and fundamentally changing the way your organization thinks about what value is to your customer and how it can drive longer-term, sustainable, and mutually beneficial relationships, start with these questions. In time, they will become second nature as everyone adapts to thinking about value as something uniquely determined by your customer and their specific situation.

SUMMARY

From the customer's perspective, everything that happens before a deal closes is at best an "appetizer." At worst, it is a necessary evil. The reason your prospect may do business with you is that they desire a future state with better outcomes than the current one. Your job is twofold: deliver on those desired outcomes and the promised value—then get credit for doing so. Only then will you be in the enviable position of having *earned the right* to ask for more business.

The first key to delivering value is understanding what "value" means to your customer. The second key is closing the right deal—that is, a deal that is not just good for both parties but one that has all the essential products and services (at the correct volumes) to allow both to deliver on that value. Finally, put in place a Customer Success Plan (or whatever you want to call it), *jointly developed* with your customer, and measure and report progress on the delivery of value through Customer Value Reviews. Now, having come full circle on the Value Lifecycle™, you've achieved a degree of competitive inoculation that is almost impossible to attain any other way!

Your job now is to manage the value you've painstakingly created to ensure that it stays fresh and relevant to your customers. Finally, to gain access to new prospects, the Value Lifecycle™ gives you critical outcome-based data to develop a Potential Value Statement, a powerful tool that can significantly increase your odds of getting an audience with key decision makers.

How do you go about turning your company into a value management machine? How can management change the conversation from an internal, product-focused view to one of value—for both your company and its customers? By "flipping" the internal conversation and asking the right questions—in the right order—of account teams. In the Appendix, I offer examples of questions that have served me well when consulting on opportunities, proposals, negotiations, and current accounts. I hope you will take and adapt them to best meet the needs of your organization.

My goal in writing this book is to help you remember that your objective is to not just win deals but rather to keep and grow customers. Therefore, delivering the value (and getting credit) is the ultimate goal, and—it bears repeating—it's also what the customer was looking for all along. As I shared at the beginning, in *Must-Win Deals*, perhaps the biggest disconnect in B2B sales today is that while customers are attempting to buy different outcomes, too often salespeople are selling to a closed deal (any closed deal) to meet *internal* quotas and goals.

When a salesperson is struggling with an anemic sales pipeline, any deal may suffice. But that much-needed sales pipeline is often hiding in plain sight within existing accounts, and these are often deals that can be quickly closed. Why don't we know about these opportunities, and why is the customer not readily offering them to us? Because we did not ensure that the value was delivered—and that credit was given to us from previous purchases.

If you follow the steps and principles in the Value Lifecycle™, I promise you an abundance of qualified opportunities. It may just make selling the best job in the world!

As a final bonus for you, I have developed a companion online workshop to this book, also named *Can't-Lose Accounts*, available online at https://mustwindeals.valuelifecycle.com. If you're interested in working on a real account by applying the concepts in these pages—something I highly recommend—please check it out. You can choose from two tiers, one that includes a standalone online workshop and a second that also includes live, one-on-one coaching from me on your Customer Success Plan. I am pleased to offer you a significant discount on either tier as a *thank you* for buying this book. Just enter the promotion code "**Book522**" to get your discount—and thanks for being a customer!

How's that for value?

Good Selling!

Questions for Changing the Conversation

Over the years, I have developed a set of questions that I ask sellers depending on where they are with their customer in the Value Lifecycle™. These are the questions I ask when brought in to consult on opportunities, proposals, negotiations, and existing accounts. I've found them to be effective regardless of my client's industry or the industry of their customer—so effective that perhaps the biggest change I've ever been asked to make was to put "achieve mission" in place of "revenue" when discussing federal, state, and local government opportunities and accounts. As a reader of this *Must-Win Deals* series, you should not be surprised that these questions are almost entirely outcome-based and customer-centric.

The *Must-Win Deals* series has been focused on managing value when interacting with the customer throughout the sales cycle, hence the term Value Lifecycle™. And while we've covered in detail the best way to manage value when you're in customer-facing situations, we've barely scratched the surface of how you should be managing value through your *internal* conversations—specifically, how frontline sales managers coach their sales teams. Why is this so important?

Humor me a bit longer if you will, and let's try another thought experiment. My intent is not to put sales management, especially frontline sales management, on the spot because I know they've arguably got the toughest job in the company. However, sales management always sets the tone for the internal, and thus external, conversations. If you are a sales rep and you have just uncovered a new opportunity, what are the first two questions sales management is likely to ask? You probably don't have to think too hard on this one: "How much is the deal for?" and "When will it close?"

I've asked this same question of hundreds of sales teams in dozens of different industries all over the world, and the response is always "How much?" and "When?" Now, to be fair to sales management, these are the two questions they know senior management will ask them, and they need the answers. But these are internal-focused, "bean counting" questions, and they're basically all "about us." How do these two questions help win more deals, make the deals larger, or help them close faster? They don't, of course. Nor could they, as they have *nothing* to do with the customer.

Additionally, recent studies show that salespeople are less extrinsically motivated than ever by things like "money." Prior to roughly 2008, 54 percent of salespeople were highly motivated by financial rewards.[10] However, the data shows that, today, half as many (no more than 27 percent) are motivated by money. Instead, they want satisfaction, praise, recognition, and fulfillment. They want to love what they do, achieve mastery, and improve the world, one customer at a time, by helping their customer become more successful. A happy customer, in other words—one that wants to renew and do more business—makes *them* happy.

How can sales management help their sales reps as well as their customers? They must change the conversation inside their teams and when coaching sales reps. How? It's all about the power of questions. As a sales rep, when you are in front of a customer, the questions you ask are one of your most powerful tools in effective selling. But for these questions

---

10   Dave Kurlan, "7 New Ways to Motivate Salespeople through 20 Old Hurdles," OMG Hub, September 8, 2014, https://www.omghub.com/salesdevelopmentblog/tabid/5809/bid/108195/7-New-Ways-to-Motivate-Salespeople-Through-20-Old-Hurdles.aspx.

to be effective, they must also come from the management level. That is, the sales rep should be asking the questions of the customer that they know their management is going to want answers to. And if they are the *right* questions, ones centered on delivering value to the customer, they can drive behavior and motivation in very positive ways. When asked, everyone will say that driving value for customers will result in better sales and business results. Yet, only 16 percent of companies execute effectively on driving value.[11] This is a huge opportunity for you to differentiate yourself and your company. What is not widely reported is that organizations that focus on driving customer value also have a more highly motivated salesforce.

QUESTIONS FOR CHANGING THE CONVERSATION

I offer the following questions as a constructive way to significantly change the sales conversation within your organization. This will facilitate driving a different (outcome- and value-focused) conversation when you or your team are in front of the customer. Additionally, these questions should

11   RAIN Group, "The Value-Driving Difference: How to Grow Revenue, Improve Win Rates, and Retain Top Sellers through Value," https://info.rainsalestraining.com/complimentary-research-report-the-value-driving-difference.

help sales management identify areas for improvement or missing key insights that can help account teams better focus their sales efforts. Let's start at the beginning of the Value Lifecycle™ when we've uncovered what appears to be a promising opportunity.

Opportunity Reviews (a.k.a. Value Creation Reviews)

As a sales manager, you arguably have one of the most difficult jobs in the company (at least it was for me in that role). You must wrangle a host of often competing (and sometimes conflicting) individuals—both within and outside your company—with the goal of keeping them all happy. This includes sales reps and account teams, senior management, customers, and channel partners. Being constantly time challenged is part of your normal day, so when you commit time to something, it better be time well spent.

Let's start at the beginning of the customer's journey (Figure A.1).

CREATING THE POTENTIAL FOR VALUE

Managing Value When Selling

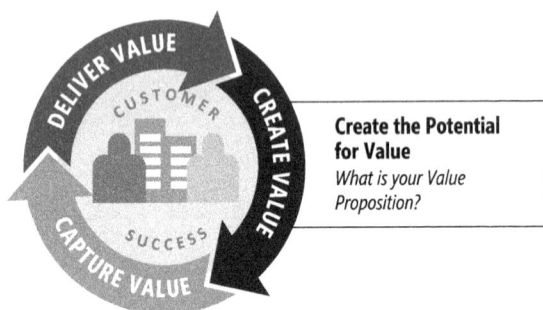

> **Create the Potential for Value**
> *What is your Value Proposition?*

Figure A.1

One of your account teams has just uncovered a significant opportunity. When they present it to you, it takes all your self-control to keep from asking, "How much?" and "When will it close?" But you refrain because you know that these are not the right questions—at least not *all* of them. Among all your responsibilities, perhaps the biggest is to coach your people to become more effective at selling, which would create scale and alleviate a lot of "fires" you currently spend much of your day putting out. You also recognize that the questions your account team expects you to ask are perhaps your greatest tool in managing and coaching effectively. But what questions should you ask at this stage of the sales cycle, when the opportunity is very immature?

Remember that the definitive output of this stage in the Value Lifecycle™ is an Irresistible Value Proposition—one that will make your customer excited about the potential of doing a deal with you and doing it quickly. Let's start with the objectives of what I call a Value Creation Review (something many find similar to an Opportunity Review). There are three primary objectives of the Value Creation Review:

→ Determine if the account team is pursuing a real deal that is the **right deal.**

→ Determine that **you can win** (and you have the best strategy to win).

→ Determine **when** the opportunity should close.

How can you best accomplish these objectives with an eye toward helping the account team position the opportunity and getting the customer excited about doing business with you? Table A.1 shows the questions I've developed over the years that I ask of teams that present me with a potential opportunity.

Use the knowledge of the entire account team and ask the following questions about their opportunity:

- What business problem(s) or opportunities are we addressing for the customer?

- What outcome(s) do they want to achieve and when?

- Who are these outcomes important to?

- How high a priority are they? How will success be measured?

- What is the customer's most likely alternative?

- Can we win, and what is our sales strategy?

- What is our Irresistible Value Proposition(s) that will compel the customer to do a deal quickly?

- What buying steps must the customer go through?

- What is our close plan to turn the opportunity into revenue, and where will the money come from?

Table A.1

Note that none of these questions is about you or the products and services you would like to sell. That's by design, as most companies need no help talking about their products and services, or themselves. Your goal is to get your account teams first talking about the things the customer cares about, which will lead to the right conversations about your products and services because they will be focused on crafting the right deal to achieve the customer's desired outcomes.

These questions are straightforward, simple, and fair. However, simple does not mean easy, and it takes a bit of practice and discipline to keep asking them, especially when you've been trained to simply answer "How much? and "When?" My experience is that the payoff is significant. As your teams begin to expect these questions, they will enter new sales campaigns knowing this is the information they need, and they will begin to have different conversations with their customers.

Proposal Reviews

Until now, we've focused on helping your account team establish that the opportunity is real, that you are aiming at the right deal, that you can win, and that your Value Proposition has motivated the customer to do business with you. Odds are, you don't have as complete and accurate a picture as you would like because of the number of buying influencers on the customer side (who are probably not all aligned), which adds to the complexity of the sale and creates significant uncertainty and risk. As such, there are two primary objectives of the Proposal Review:

→ Determine what is causing **uncertainty** and **risk**.

→ Determine how to make it easier to **buy from you** (and sell internally).

You will ultimately accomplish these with a Compelling Proposal. Figure A.2 shows where the account team is in the Value Lifecycle™.

THE COMPELLING OUTCOME-BASED PROPOSAL
The Crucial Bridge Between Selling and Negotiating

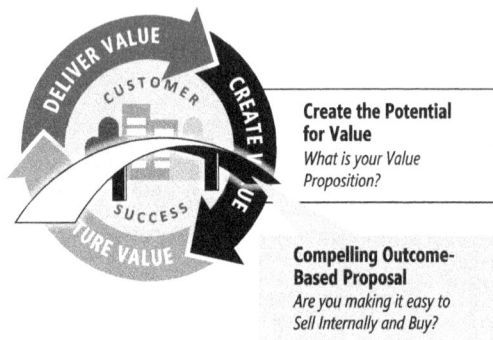

Create the Potential for Value
What is your Value Proposition?

Compelling Outcome-Based Proposal
Are you making it easy to Sell Internally and Buy?

Figure A.2

We discussed the components of the seven-slide proposal at length in *The Compelling Proposal*. Here, I would like to focus on the heart of the approach, Multiple Acceptable Options (MAOs), as this is where I find account teams generally need the most help in developing the right options for this specific selling situation. MAOs both manage the uncertainty and allow the customer to "buy" from you (and feel it is the right decision for them).

Table A.2 shows the questions I ask account teams when helping them develop their options.

Use the knowledge of the entire account team and ask the following questions about their proposal.

- What are we uncertain about?

- Is the customer presenting us with conflicting demands or priorities?

- Does our sales strategy for this customer include future upsell and cross-sell opportunities?

- How might we structure options to address the uncertainties, overcome conflicting priorities, and/or advance our long-term strategy?

Table A.2

This is where sales management can bring significant value to the account team in helping them construct the right options for this customer and this situation. Remember, all the options must be acceptable to you because the customer may actually choose one of them (no "stinkers" or red herrings). However, nine times out of ten, the final deal is more likely to be a combination of options. Skillfully constructed, the options will generate *the right dialogue and the right negotiation* with the customer.

By inviting the customer to participate in discussing and evaluating the pros and cons of these options, you are also encouraging them to take ownership of "their deal," one they help construct. This can have the effect of compressing sales cycles, sometimes dramatically, as your customer is able to more easily sell "their deal" internally—and they will be motivated to do so. Now, you've done everything in your power to set up the right negotiation.

Negotiation Reviews (a.k.a. Value Capture Reviews)

The formal negotiation is another key pressure point in the sales cycle the sales manager should help the account team prepare for. As we discussed in *The Painless Negotiation*, you've actually been negotiating from the very beginning of the sales campaign by anchoring the sale and negotiation. However, many large enterprises will insist that you also deal with procurement in a separate, formal negotiation. Figure A.3 shows where we are in the Value Lifecycle™.

CAPTURE VALUE IN A GREAT DEAL
Managing Value When Negotiating

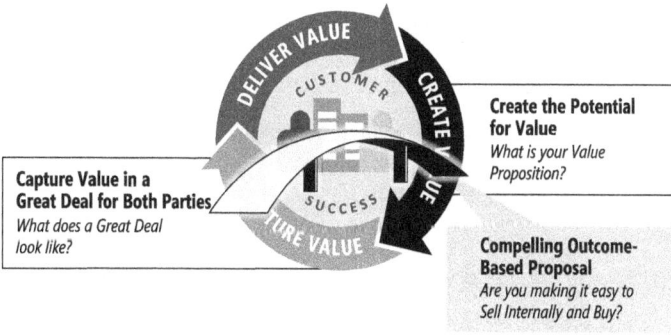

Figure A.3

Your goal is to capture the value you've created in a great deal, one that is good for the customer, good for you, and contains all the key deal levers to allow both parties to ultimately deliver the promised value. If the account team is not aiming at a great deal, then what are they prepared to accept? Often, it means they will accept *any deal* (as long as it closes before the end of the quarter). This is what you must guard against. To prepare the account team for the formal negotiation, you need to ensure they understand the dynamics at play and have a negotiation plan. The two objectives you want to achieve are:

→ Ensure you are having the **right negotiation.**

→ Prepare the team to negotiate the **right way.**

The simple set of questions I routinely ask account teams to prepare them for the negotiation are shown in Table A.3.

Use the knowledge of the entire account team and ask the following questions about their negotiation plan.

- Based on each side's most likely alternatives, how compelling is a deal and which side has the power in this negotiation?

- Are we aligned internally on the right deal levers, priorities, and limits for this opportunity (internal negotiation)? What levers will be easy to negotiate, and which ones will require trading?

- How do we intend to anchor the sale and negotiation, and what anchors by the other side must we manage?

- What tactics have they used in the past? What do we expect the other side to do this time? What are we prepared to trade in response?

Table A.3

You obviously want the team prepared to manage expected customer negotiation tactics and have the foundational insights to deal with unexpected tactics. The better prepared the team is to negotiate the deal, the better the odds they will negotiate confidently and close a higher-quality deal quickly. Obviously, you can't predict every tactic that procurement may use (except for one—see the sidebar), but you can better prepare your team for the formal negotiation.

Account Reviews (a.k.a. Value Delivery Reviews)

Sales organizations typically give existing customers a lot of pro-forma attention using formal account plans at the beginning of the fiscal year. My issue with most account planning is that it is treated as an "event," and the account plan is soon on the shelf gathering dust. These plans also focus too much on *what we want to sell them* rather than what the customer may be interested in buying. But if we have failed to deliver the promised value from previous purchases and get credit for that value, none of this may matter. That's where the Value Delivery Review comes in.

Figure A.4 shows where we are in the Value Lifecycle™.

DELIVERING VALUE AND GETTING CREDIT

Managing Value After the Sale

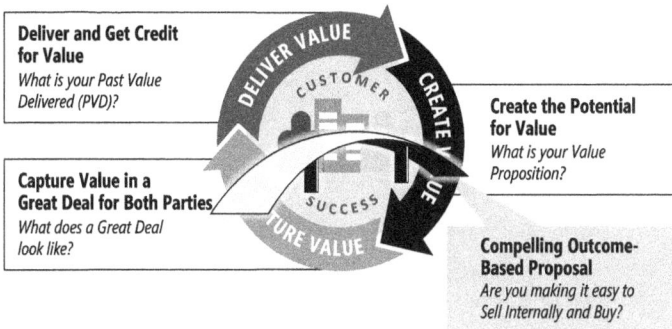

Deliver and Get Credit for Value
What is your Past Value Delivered (PVD)?

Capture Value in a Great Deal for Both Parties
What does a Great Deal look like?

Create the Potential for Value
What is your Value Proposition?

Compelling Outcome-Based Proposal
Are you making it easy to Sell Internally and Buy?

Figure A.4

After contract award, from a sales perspective you want to sell more products and services in the future to this customer. Recognizing that the easiest sale in the world is to an existing, *happy* customer, the two key objectives for a Value Delivery Review are:

→ Ensure you have **delivered the promised value** (and been given **credit**).

→ Uncover and manage what is **changing** with the customer's business.

Let's now turn our attention to the simple set of questions I routinely ask account teams by way of conducting a Value Delivery Review and developing an account plan, as shown in Table A.4.

Use the knowledge of the entire account team and ask the following questions about their account.

- How does the customer use our products and services to operate their business today?

- What is the relevant Past Value Delivered (PVD) we have been given credit for? Who has given us credit?

- How has the customer's business changed, and what business issues/opportunities does this present to the customer now?

- Who are these changes important to, and why?

- What new sales opportunities might this present to us, and how will we pursue them to create value?

Table A.4

You are now right back where you started, creating the potential for value for the customer for *new* sales opportunities—and the Value Lifecycle™ goes on and on. I hope these questions have given you some ideas for how you might shift your internal conversations away from an inside-out view to a much more outside-in view of the customer and what is truly important to them. By no means are these all the questions you might ask, but I've found they are a big help in quickly getting to the heart of the matter, depending on where the account team and customer are in the Value Lifecycle™. At a minimum, they should be a good place to start for frontline sales managers!

Case Story Customer Success Plan

Agile
INFORMATION SOLUTION

MFS
MEGA FINANCIAL SYSTEMS

MFS Customer Success Plan:

Integrate the Worldwide and AIC

Acquisitions Ahead of Board Deadline

Paul Stockard – Account Manager

November 2, 2020

Focus Areas	Outcomes / Metrics	Value Delivered	Notes / Action Items
Worldwide / MFS Integration	Compile and Reformat MFS Account Data by 10/12/20	Completed 10/11/20 ahead of schedule	None
	Import MFS Account Data by 10/19/20	Completed 10/15/20 ahead of schedule	None
	Rebrand Worldwide Platform, Portal, and Interfaces to MFS by 10/23/20	Completed 10/20/20 ahead of schedule	None
	Train MFS Sales on Worldwide Platform, Portal, and Interfaces by 10/24/20	Completed 10/23/20 on schedule	None
	MFS IT Manage Agile Platform by 11/2/20	Scheduled for 11/30/20 - Delayed	Hire for IT Staff Turnover
	Go Live (100% Uptime) by 10/26/2)	Platform Live on 10/23/20 (100% Uptime)	None
AIC Integration	Compile and Reformat AIC Account Data by 11/2/20	Completed 10/28/20 ahead of schedule	None
	Import AIC Account Data by 11/9/20	Ahead of schedule for Import on 11/5/20	Daily Tracking
	Complete "Hot Updates" – Zero Downtime	2 Hot Updates 10/28/20 (100% Uptime)	Included Platform Upgrade
	AIC Go Live on MFS by 11/9/20	Ahead of schedule for Go Live on 11/5/20	Daily Tracking

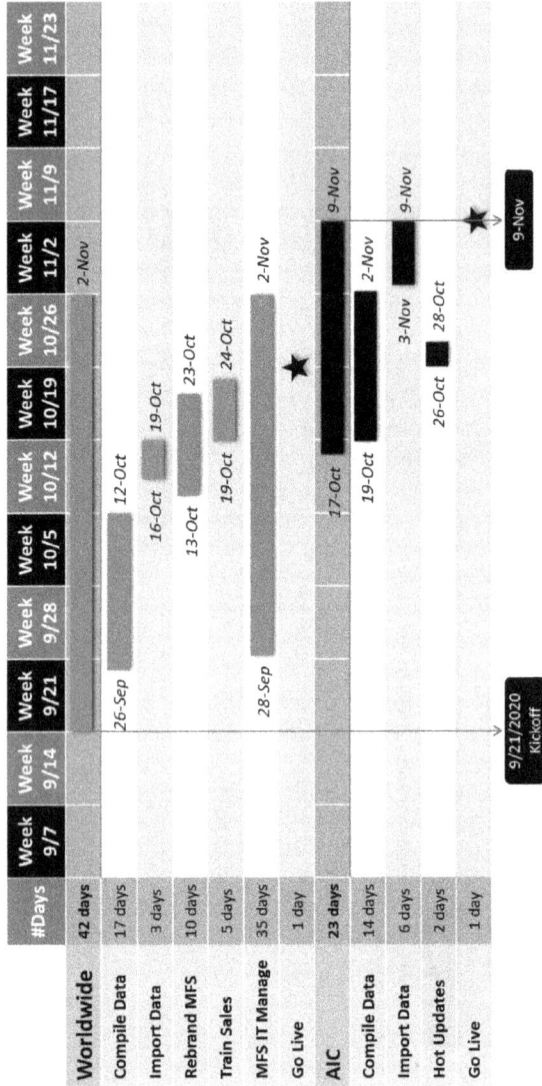

MFS Implementation Plan

Ag*i*le

	#Days	Week 9/7	Week 9/14	Week 9/21	Week 9/28	Week 10/5	Week 10/12	Week 10/19	Week 10/26	Week 11/2	Week 11/9	Week 11/17	Week 11/23
Worldwide	42 days												
Compile Data	17 days			26-Sep		12-Oct							
Import Data	3 days					16-Oct	19-Oct						
Rebrand MFS	10 days						13-Oct	23-Oct					
Train Sales	5 days						19-Oct	24-Oct					
MFS IT Manage	35 days			28-Sep					2-Nov				
Go Live	1 day												
AIC	23 days					17-Oct				9-Nov			
Compile Data	14 days					19-Oct			2-Nov				
Import Data	6 days								3-Nov	9-Nov			
Hot Updates	2 days							26-Oct	28-Oct				
Go Live	1 day									9-Nov			

9/21/2020 Kickoff

9-Nov

Changes and Innovations

Focus Areas	Change / Innovation	Responsible (Agile & MFS)	Action Items
Changes	Staff Attrition of MFS IT Engineers	D. Hand / S. Renly	Reschedule Platform Training – **DONE**
	Agile Engineers Staff Augmentation Support for MFS IT	P. Stockard / S. Holder	Through 11/30/20 – **DONE**
	Hiring of MFS IT Engineers	J. Jones / S. Renly	8 of 10 Hired – **IN PROCESS**
	Extend Platform Training Scope	P. Stockard / S. Holder	Extend through 11/30/20 – **DONE**
Innovations	Dataccess Cloud Platform Update Version 13.18.25 Available 10/15/18	D. Hand / S. Renly, M. Sorenson	Schedule Dataccess Platform Upgrade – **DONE**
	Updated Integration Scoping Process	D. Hand / M. Sorenson	Train MFS IT Staff and Implement on AIC – **DONE**
	Re-Platforming Process Update / Revision	D. Hand / M. Sorenson	Testing on AIC Integration – **IN PROCESS**

Communications Plan

Agile

- **Daily Meetings** (Detailed Implementation Planning)
  - D. Hand, J. Jones / S. Renly, M. Sorenson

- **Weekly Meetings** (Implementation Status Review)
  - D. Hand, J. Jones, P. Stockard / S. Renly, M. Sorenson, B. Sellers

- **Customer Value Reviews** (Value Delivered after Worldwide & AIC Integrations)
  - P. Stockard, T. Rosser
  - S. Renly, B. Sellers

Next CVR: January 12, 2021, at 9:00 A.M.

www.ingramcontent.com/pod-product-compliance
Lightning Source LLC
Chambersburg PA
CBHW031859200326
41597CB00012B/475